AFTER DANIEL

AFTER DANIEL

A SUICIDE
SURVIVOR'S
TALE

MOIRA FARR

Harper*Flamingo*Canada

AFTER DANIEL: A SUICIDE SURVIVOR'S TALE
Copyright © 1999 by Moira Farr.
All rights reserved. No part of this book may be used or reproduced in any manner what-
soever without prior written permission except in the case of brief quotations embodied
in reviews. For information address HarperCollins Publishers Ltd, Suite 2900, Hazelton
Lanes, 55 Avenue Road, Toronto, Canada M5R 3L2.

http://www.harpercanada.com

HarperCollins books may be purchased for educational, business, or sales promotional
use. For information please write: Special Markets Department, HarperCollins Canada,
Suite 2900, Hazelton Lanes, 55 Avenue Road, Toronto, Canada M5R 3L2.

First HarperCollins hardcover ed. ISBN 0-00-255725-8
First HarperCollins trade paper ed. ISBN 0-00-638479-X

First Edition

Canadian Cataloguing in Publication Data

Farr, Moira, 1958-
After Daniel: a suicide survivor's tale

Includes bibliographical references.
ISBN 0-00-255725-8

1. Farr, Moira, 1958-. 2. Suicide. I. Title
HV6545.F37 1999   362.28'092   C99-930449-6

99 00 01 02 03 04 HC 8 7 6 5 4 3 2 1

Printed and bound in the United States

For all my friends, living and dead

*Everything the dead predicted has turned out
completely different.
Or a little bit different—which is to say,
completely different.*

— From "The Letters of the Dead," by Wislawa Szymborska
(translated by Stanislaw Baranczak
and Clare Cavanagh)

*I seek out the horror which, like history itself, can't be
stanched. I read everything I can. My eagerness for details is
offensive.*

— From *Fugitive Pieces*, by Anne Michaels

*And when there is the promise of a storm, if you want change
in your life, walk into it. If you get on the other side, you will
be different. And if you want change in your life and you are
avoiding the trouble, you can forget it. So . . . wade on in the
water, it's going to really be troubled water.*

— From *Sweet Honey in the Rock, Live at Carnegie Hall, 1986*,
introduction to "Wade In The Water" (traditional)

PROLOGUE

1993. A WARM EVENING, LATE IN SPRING. A man and a woman, casually dressed, in their thirties, sit across from each other in a small, shabby-chic Latin American restaurant on Queen Street West in Toronto, the kind with rough, painted walls where the work of local starving artists is always on display. Their table is at the front of the narrow, candle-lit place, surrounded by the current selection of abstract murals, near the big full-length windows, now de rigueur in the city's bars and restaurants, swung open to take in the balmy air and offer the framed Saturday-night scene of the restaurant's inviting interior to any curious passersby.

When they order, the young man reaches across the table and touches her hand lightly. "You can have a drink, you know. It doesn't bother me." It's thoughtful of him. She had been wondering about the etiquette of consuming alcohol in the company of someone who has had to give it up; in the company of an alcoholic, that is. Assured that it is acceptable, she orders a glass of wine, he a diet soft drink. They share a plate of fresh mussels in a spicy tomato sauce.

The city is experiencing its first taste of summer—the suddenly, unequivocally warm weather that, in northern climates, seems to raise an entire population's basic happiness level a notch or two.

After months of hunkering down indoors, making only reluctant forays outside, bundled in cumbersome coats, hats, gloves, and boots, trudging through a dreary urban landscape eternally clad in shades of grey, black, and brown, people are out in exuberant droves as they renounce their winter clothing with sweet relief. There's a heavy, sensual mugginess in the air this night, and an almost festive energy along the café-lined streets of the downtown's west end as people whiz by on bikes and in-line skates, or stroll along the sidewalks looking for somewhere to sit for a meal or a drink, preferably outdoors or by an open window. Bits of conversation and laughter float into the little restaurant, mingling with the low buzz of the people at various tables and hunched on stools around the curved bar.

The man and woman sit talking and watching the passing scene long after their plates have been cleared away. The restaurant is less crowded now, approaching midnight, and the street too. The moist air has entered that electrically charged state of stillness that precedes thunderous downpours. A rolling grey cover of clouds has taken over the sky. The breeze is gathering force, bringing with it ominously spaced drops, and soon, slow splashes of rain through the restaurant's windows. A waiter asks the man and woman if they would like him to close the windows, but they say, no, it's okay. They're just enjoying the warm wind blowing in on them, thunder sounding in the distance. The rain splashes onto the woman's hand as it rests on the table. The coolness of it feels fine, she doesn't brush it away. The back of the man's shirt is speckled wet, that seems fine too. He says he could make them iced coffees back at his place, and she says, great. As they leave, the clouds release their rain and finally it pounds down on the city, a welcome deluge after a long, dry spell.

As they emerge onto the street the man opens an umbrella, putting his arm around the woman's shoulders. Together they run, west and north through Bellwoods Park. It's the first time they've been this physically close. The woman is keenly aware of it; they have been hovering tentatively on the brink of intimacy for some time now. When they first met for coffee months earlier, he was ending a marriage he said had been going bad for years. Now he is separated, and she is not sure what she wants. The last couple of times they've been out, she has thought that he might have expected her to invite him in when he walks her to her door, but she doesn't. The last time, she was all too conscious of her growing nervousness over what might happen next, and her anxious blathering to cover it, as they approached the street where she lived. But he seems sensitive to her diffidence, with no intention of pushing his luck, and they say an awkward, shuffling *Um, well, guess I'll see you then, well, uh, should I call you, uh sure, I guess so, okay, ha ha, well, see you then, bye.* The man would later tease her about her obvious skittishness. "You were running," he tells her, insisting she had turned on her heels and loped away from him that evening, though she thinks this is an exaggeration. By his account, he continued on up the street, feeling sure she'd never go out with him again, lamenting what he presumed was his lack of finesse with women.

She's not sure what prompted her to keep her distance, apart from the psychotherapeutically correct notion that people just out of relationships are more vulnerable than they know, more likely to make hasty romantic choices clouded by wounded loneliness. Maybe she has been waiting for him to blow it, in some hopeless, bad-date cliché: rant about his ex; attempt to sell her Amway products; tell her in detail about his corkscrew collection; allude to his Hefneresque sexual prowess; dismiss any opinion of hers with which he disagrees; confess to, or unconsciously exhibit, some sickening habit; tell her fifteen minutes into their first coffee together that he is really a loner who doesn't like commitment and has never had a relationship that lasted longer than three weeks.

He does none of these things. No, to her, it all looks better, not worse, the more time they spend together. Of course, there are all the obvious common interests, the writing and editing and reading, plenty of easy shop talk. But it's more than that, a good feeling she has with him, that he understands things, without her having to explain. They've both been through dark times, they are quite open about their pasts; they both want to leave the painful things behind, get on with better lives.

Now they're in the park. The downpour has stopped, but the man still gallantly holds the umbrella over their heads. They trot along, their new physical closeness making them politely reserved once again, mindlessly chattering. The woman begins to wonder if he is ever going to notice the umbrella is no longer necessary. Then it strikes her as terribly funny, and she can't help it, she breaks away and runs on a little, laughing the way people do when they have been holding it in, when their laughter may be a distracting cover for some deeper emotion. "Daniel, it's not raining anymore!" she calls back. "Oh," he says, looking befuddled, "you're right." He catches up with her, and somehow, in all the dithering over closing the umbrella, he manages to lean down and kiss her. It is a rather shy, perhaps-we-should-get-this-out-of-the-way-so-we-can-both-relax kind of kiss. Not since high school can she remember feeling such awkwardness, and she is not sure how to account for it. Still, it seems now they can relax, and they walk on, in the damp night air, a fine mist visibly suspended in the light pooling around the streetlamps.

At his place, she kicks off her new clogs, and looks down to see with dismay that the dye from their dark leather tops has run in the rain, staining her feet a bruisy black and blue, as though she's been stomping through a vat of grapes. She sits at the kitchen table while he makes the coffee, curling her feet self-consciously underneath the chair, as the talk flows easily between them. Finally, she makes what she knows must sound like a strange request: "Would you mind if I washed my feet?" An obliging and gracious host, he replies, "Of course not." She thanks him, enters the tiny bathroom, runs some water in the scarred old tub, sits on its edge, and dips her feet in.

Soon he is behind her with a towel, but instead of giving it to her, he sits down and drapes it over the tub beside him. He has also brought soap. He puts his hand in the water to test its temperature, then gently takes one of her feet and begins, silently, with great care and concentration, to wash away the stain. "Oh," is all she can think to say.

Something extraordinary seems to happen between them. She can hardly express its quality. Perhaps it's rare to be able to trace the precise moment when a relationship changes from one thing into another, from casual to serious, from unattached to bonded. For her, this tender ritual marks one such moment. It sets a pattern, for this man and woman; their silences, she finds, are as rich, vital, and connected as their conversations.

What she starts to feel is a magnificent sense of calm. She cannot remember the last time she experienced such intense intimacy. Maybe she has never felt it, not like this. She rests her head on his shoulder, immensely filled with a sense of arrival, after a long and painful journey; how amazing to have arrived at each other, hardly knowing before they got here that it was a possible destination. She feels safe, welcome, cherished. Home. Healing already. She feels she could stay like this, accepted, comforted, loved by this man forever.

A beautiful memory, now juxtaposed with so many terrible ones. The summer dream that veered so abruptly and disastrously into the nightmare of the following winter. Sitting side by side with him that evening as he—Daniel—gently washed her feet, it would have been impossible to imagine how quickly she would become the one administering the care, inconceivable that he would be capable of destroying himself, hurting her so badly, leaving her— that is, me, for this is a true story, my story—so soon, so tragically.

Now, I sometimes wonder, as I run that exquisite evening through my memory—the indelible image of Daniel, strong and peaceful beside me—how it is that a man capable of such a sweetly inspired gesture could also contain within himself such overpowering shame and rage and self-loathing. I wonder, looking back, to whom, and for what, he was in some way always unconsciously atoning.

He cannot tell me. I am left to wonder that for the rest of my life.

On February 13th, 1994, Daniel Jones, the man I loved, killed himself, employing a method outlined in the bestselling manual of "self deliverance," *Final Exit.* He was one month short of his thirty-fifth birthday; a recovered alcoholic who had not had a drink in eight years; a man who had struggled for a long time to keep his deeply rooted depression and agoraphobia at bay; a gifted writer, editor, collector of books; a generous friend; a demanding and self-chastising perfectionist; a withering critic of pretense, hypocrisy, and mediocrity; a fine, loving companion.

I use the term "killed himself" to describe what Daniel did, as opposed to "committed suicide," "took his own life," "died by his own hand," or other such distanced phrasings, because for me it most aptly expresses the particular violence that it takes for a young man nowhere near the end of his natural life to cause his own death—especially a young man who also possessed such rare tenderness of spirit. If ever there was a man who contained his opposites, it was Daniel. The day he died, it was as though the tectonic plates of my entire existence shifted, causing all my assumptions and understanding of what it means to know someone, my sense of life's meaning and purpose, to fall to the rumbling ground. I've spent the five years since shaking off the initial daze of that cataclysm, learning how to navigate the strange, new coordinates of my altered world.

I could, and do occasionally, refer to the act in conventional terms—the act in general, for Daniel is only one of many who have chosen to die this way—as "committing suicide." Unless quoting someone, or distinguishing between attempted and successful suicides, I will avoid referring to it as "completing suicide," a relatively new term that I find stilted, though I respect the efforts of those in the field of suicide prevention who wish to steer our language and cultural understanding away from the criminality implied by the word "commit." Suicide is no longer a felony in most countries, including Canada—though I do know of at least one clergyman who was called upon as recently as the early seventies to visit a man sent to Toronto's Don Jail for slashing his wrists.

No, I most often conceive of what Daniel did as killing himself, because saying it that way best evokes the full horror of the act and hearkens back to why our ancestors, motivated by primal fears, fashioned fierce social taboos around suicide, and called it "self-murder." This I understand. I believe there was as much rage as there was despair in Daniel's suicidal drive, a will to die that required energy and force to execute successfully; ironic, given the depressive's characteristic listlessness and outright emotional paralysis, and Daniel was nothing if not depressive for a good part of his short life.

"Commiting" or "completing" suicide strikes me as altogether too tidy a way of describing something that can be—before, during and after—an outrageous mess. Yes, some planning and rationality, not to mention rationalization, are often involved in carrying out the act, aside from cases in which extreme derangement, psychosis, or schizophrenic delusion drives a person to self-inflicted death. Suicidal people may knowingly mask from others the degree of their pain and the extent of their self-destructive plans, or they may act impulsively. Yet, at the heart of suicide is most often a chaos of distorted perception and emotion that leads the afflicted person on a doomed chase down a dark, lonely, and mistaken path. By that point of isolation, there's usually no one who can stop it from happening; no one who fully understands that there is something that needs to be stopped from happening.

In ending his own life, Daniel brought immeasurable grief and sorrow into the lives of many people. If he was desperately seeking the peace of oblivion, he did so at the expense of the living. Still, I do not judge him. He was sensitive enough to know how much he would hurt others, and apologized in his suicide note for the pain and suffering his death would cause. He is forgiven, by me anyway, and I believe by most who knew and loved him.

Since I am a writer, it is, I suppose, not surprising that I would write about such a profound and traumatic experience as the suicide of a lover. Yet my own loss has not been the sole impetus for my writing this book, though it is, without question, at the heart of it. No, it was more a combination of events and circumstances in the wake of Daniel's suicide that made me feel I was somehow called upon—in the right or wrong place at the right or wrong time, I think—to begin seeing the world in a different light. I knew I could never go back to the old way of seeing, or not seeing. To do so would have been cheating myself and possibly others experiencing their own suicide tragedies.

Shortly after Daniel's death, I learned that a former classmate of mine from journalism school had also killed himself—only days before Daniel, as it happened—though others kept the news from me for many weeks, assuming correctly that I would have been unable to take it in. The news rattled me anyway, when it did come one day in early April 1994. For me, it was a chilling time, the height of the media frenzy over the suicide of grunge-rock icon Kurt Cobain. I felt as if I had entered some dangerous and inescapable echo chamber, where my own thoughts and concerns were painfully amplified no matter which way I turned. Then, in June, I learned that another close friend had lost a good friend to suicide; picking up the phone and getting this news, I felt as though the wind were being kicked out of me. What was going on? Why did so many of us have to grieve so painfully and profoundly these untimely deaths? What could end these cycles of misery?

I found these questions maddeningly difficult to answer. As I sought to bring some sense and order to it all, I could not help noting that Daniel, my old schoolmate, and my friend's friend were all thirty-four years old, male, introspective, creative types who had long suffered varying combinations and degrees of depression, substance abuse, and family dysfunction. Cobain fit this mold too, though dying somewhat younger, at twenty-seven. Discerning this characteristic destructive pattern was one of the first steps I took to place my own experience in a larger perspective; it was the beginning of the healing search that became this book.

If all I sought to do here was to enact some personal therapy (and I don't deny that a project such as this includes that kind of catharsis), I would keep my reflections in the pages of a diary, and there would not be much point in sharing them with anyone. But suicide seems to bring out a literary urge in many who experience it. Memoirs by suicide survivors* have been written, chiefly by mothers mourning dead sons, though other kinds of loss experiences are now emerging too, and I was grateful to have such enlightening and compassionate company as I traversed my own grief. In Canada alone, a retired judge has written a moving book of poetry since the suicide of his wife (*Silver Mercies,* by James Clarke), and so has a woman whose severely schizophrenic son killed himself in a terrible and violent episode of delusion (*The Unhinging of Wings,* by Margo Button). The American actor Spalding Gray based his famous monologue *Monster in a Box* on his experience of surviving the suicide of his mother. The monster of the title is the massive, unfinishable novel about this suicide in Gray's young adulthood that tyrannizes his emotional life. Many suicide survivors will nod and smile in recognition at Gray's self-portrait of a man who, years after failing (in his own neurotic

* The term now commonly used to describe those who have lost loved ones to suicide, though technically, it could apply to those who have survived suicide attempts. Unless specifically noted, I will from here on use the term in reference to the former group.

view) to prevent the suicide of a loved one, volunteers to work the distress–phone lines on Christmas Day, expiating his guilt in some poignant and unconscious hope that he can redeem his own loss by saving someone else. Gray is ultimately wise enough to understand that it doesn't quite work that way.

I also found specialized literature on suicide and bereavement among survivors helpful as I tried to come to terms with the event in my own life. (See the end of this book for a list of suggested reading.) But it disturbed me, as I read, that most people likely to read or even to be aware of these works would be those who had a personal or professional reason to do so. Others without such a close connection to suicide gain their impressions and understanding of the subject mainly from media coverage that is often distorted by clichés, misconceptions, and simplistic analyses that do not begin to encompass the complexities of each instance of suicide. Leftover fears stemming from old-style religious attitudes, and deeply rooted urges to stigmatize and silence in some families and communities, combine to fuel a collective ignorance that actually endangers our health.

I became aware that my own obsession with the subject—my burning need to know, in intricate and complete detail, why this suicide had happened—represented a common grief reaction among people who have survived a traumatic loss, and in particular, a suicide. I suppose I eventually rationalized, through some deep-seated Presbyterian impulse, that if I must have an obsession, I would at least be putting it to good use in writing a book, transforming chaos into reason and purpose. I wrestled with the unavoidable: To get beyond such a devastating experience paradoxically I had to immerse myself in it; to find a new reason for hope and optimism in my life, I had to steel myself, stand up, and stare down this monstrous thing called suicide. In a culture that doesn't want to understand it, but likes to titillate itself with little media samplings and fictitious or cinematic smatterings of it, I would be exposed to it anyway, whether I liked it or not. Despite setbacks and dark times I would not have thought I had the strength to get through, what began as a typical mourner's quest to understand why people kill themselves eventually became an exploration of why I, and countless others, do not.

This would be a good place to dispel an unfortunate and limiting notion: that to think, talk, or write about suicide is inherently depressing and therefore best avoided. When some suggested that I must be crazy to willingly expose myself to the world of suicide in researching and writing such a book, they seemed to suggest that it would be healthier to bury the grief (I tried, unsuccesfully), scurry away from all mention of this tragic reality, and skip off into the sunset without looking back.

It's that cut-and-run approach I now find more depressing. It leads nowhere honest, cannot enhance understanding, or allow forgiveness and resolution. The attitude plays into an inadequate and well-entrenched style of coping and grieving. Those in the growing field of bereavement counselling and support are only beginning to effectively dismantle the attitude that says the best way to deal with a painful experience is to erase it from your mind as quickly as possible, as though it had never occurred at all, as though you should reject the task of mourning altogether. Anyone dealing with trauma faces the temptation of going this route. It sometimes happens without the afflicted individual even recognizing it: Delayed grief over a major loss is fairly common. Certainly, there are enough social forces at large that would have us smile though our hearts are breaking, putting on a show for the benefit of others, long before grief is truly resolved—a process that can take years. Yet facing the enormity of our losses fully and openly, and never failing to appreciate them, means we are in fact less likely to get stuck in our grief, and more likely to integrate it into our lives, avoiding either extreme of denial or obsession. Only in acknowledging the presence of loss do we gain control over the reality of tragic absence.

With this book, I hope to contribute to a larger discussion and understanding of suicide and the mourning that it necessitates, one that includes not only professionals and survivors, but also people who are likely to experience it at least indirectly—for suicide, after all, is as old and as widespread as humanity itself. References to it and expressions of despair go back to the beginnings of history; one of the classic texts of our own century is Albert Camus's *The Myth of Sisyphus*, in which the philosopher explores the age-old question "To be, or not to be?" judging it *the* question that every seeker of truth must ask in order to start pushing against the meaning of life. Camus concludes that while life is essentially absurd, the moral person chooses to live it anyway, and rejects suicide as a rational or meaningful response to life's cosmic absurdity.

While the vast majority of human souls do choose to live, many will contemplate suicide at some point, whether as part of some fundamental philosophical questioning, or out of a more deeply felt sense of personal anguish. Even Freud expressed suicidal feelings as a young man, in a distraught letter to his wife-to-be during their courtship, when he suggested that he would kill himself if she rejected him. The conditions, circumstances, and triggers for suicide and suicidal feelings may be ever in flux across times and cultures, but the urge toward self-destruction, and its attendant feelings of despair, are timeless and universal.

There are many fascinating facts about suicide at the disposal of anyone who wants to look at them, and for a time I did, looking for connections and explanations. I learned many things: That the highest suicide rate in the world is in Siberia, which recently edged out Hungary, the longstanding holder of that dubious accolade. The lowest rate is in Greece; no one seems to know why, though speculation is entertaining. The only place in the world where women kill themselves in greater numbers than men is China. Everywhere else, roughly two-thirds of suicides are men; firearms are the most common means they employ. Women attempt suicide more often than men, but succeed less frequently because they tend to opt for less lethal means, such as pills.

Right now, in Canada, the highest rates of suicide are found among the country's most marginalized population, the aboriginal community. In fact, in 1996, statistics showed that aboriginal men in Canada had the highest suicide rate of any demographically defined group in the world. Coincidence? I think not. It doesn't require a genius, let alone a psychiatrist, to realize that a problem of this magnitude, with such deep historical and cultural roots, will not be solved solely by regulating the flow of the chemical serotonin through individually treated brains. To imagine so is an affront to the humanity of many suffering souls: "Let them take Prozac" is not an adequate response to this scale of tragedy.

Antidepressants may be a useful tool in a person's fighting arsenal against depression, and the suicidal feelings that can attend it, but they cannot vanquish such feelings altogether. Daniel had been taking such medications faithfully for years at the time of his death. Despite the advent of these drugs and public prevention and education programs, suicide rates are not going down, and in some countries and communities, they are even going up. Given global suicide statistics showing that roughly 2,000 people kill themselves every day, not many of us will go through our lives without being exposed in some way to at least one such death.

Those who deal with people traumatized by suicide are also beginning to acknowledge that you don't have to be closely related to the deceased to experience feelings of confusion and loss. It's less unusual now for a variety of people beyond family and friends to seek counselling after witnessing or being in some proximity to a suicide: the colleagues of the business executive who hangs himself in his office; the taxi driver who drives a passenger to a requested spot, then watches in horror as the man leaves the cab and shoots himself in the head; the random passerby who happens upon someone jumping to her death from a high bridge; the person driving beneath whose car narrowly misses the falling body; the school janitor who finds the boy hanging in a dark supply room; the credit counsellor who in the course of a seven-year practice has twelve clients commit suicide and many others attempt it. All true stories.

As I struggled through my own grief, reflected, read, witnessed, I became more acutely aware that as a society, we often give lip service to the notion that human life is precious, yet everywhere and every day, new evidence arises that we don't really value it as highly as we claim. "We live in a culture that encourages us not to take our own suffering seriously," writes the wise Alice Miller in her ground-breaking book *The Drama of the Gifted Child.* The taboo around suicide in particular still exerts its force. Ironically, that is perhaps why I had no trouble finding people willing to share their own experiences with me; it was as though many had had little opportunity to discuss the event and their feelings surrounding it. Mostly, it was through word of mouth that I met the people I interviewed: friends of friends, colleagues, someone who knew someone who. The more I heard their stories, the more I was convinced that such profound experiences should not remain invisible.

It was astonishing, and very moving, to observe and be on the receiving end of this brimming need to talk. Strangers revealed to me the most extraordinary and painful things: families that had endured multiple suicides; grief unexperienced for years, bursting out with great force when least expected; years of lies and silence over deaths never acknowledged as suicides. It would be tough, and a disservice, to generalize about the deceased people who haunted these heartfelt conversations, except in one sense: All emerged as damaged, in one way or another, as people who had for some reason—many reasons—not developed, or had lost for a crucial time the skills to cope with adversity, or just the challenges of everyday existence.

Without people coming forward and telling their stories, it would have been difficult for me to make the necessary connections, and for all of us to build the knowledge required to help prevent future tragedies. Only now are the roots of what is termed" suicidality" becoming more widely understood; only now is understanding the experience of surviving suicide recognized as a crucial part of under-standing the nature of suicide itself.

In the initial chapters of this book, I describe how it was for me in the first moments, days, and months after discovering Daniel had killed himself. I do this because often when suicide is depicted, we see and experience only the shock of the suicidal moment, a little hit of horror, and then the curtain falls and we hustle along, preferring not to see what happens next. Perhaps if we lingered awhile and witnessed the effects of these suicides on the people who must now live with the aftershocks—those who, statistically, are themselves at higher risk for suicide after having experienced one— we would place more value on prevention and be more serious about coming to terms with such problems as undiagnosed or poorly treated mental illness, addictions of every kind, family dysfunction, the emotional and physical abuse of children, economic and social dislocation, and the wide proliferation of guns.

We need to enhance our overall cultural literacy in all matters regarding the damaged souls society can't seem to stop producing, and the ways in which it is made easier for them to solve their problems through self-imposed death. After thirty years of serious research in the field now known as "suicidology," much knowledge does exist about what causes, and what could prevent, suicide. But more people need to know of it, and to know the importance of knowing it. Like most Canadians, I was totally unaware that our country boasts the largest archive of literature about suicide in the world, the Suicide Information and Education Centre in Calgary, Alberta, until I began work on this book.

In the course of my own recovery and research, I became a volunteer counsellor to other survivors, read extensively, saved clippings, noted my own reactions to various suicides, attended conferences, met with inmates at the Drumheller Institution in Alberta, the first group to run a wholly inmate-directed suicide-prevention program in Canada. I also visited a crisis-intervention worker on a reserve with one of the highest suicide rates in the country, spoke with a rabbi in a midtown Toronto synagogue, and attended a

Blackfoot sweat ceremony in the foothills of the Rockies southwest of Calgary. I interviewed the parents of three teenage boys who had killed themselves in police custody. During a conference of the American Association of Suicidology, in Memphis, Tennessee, I toured Graceland with a vanload of shrinks, psychologists, and social workers. In Toronto, I attended a weird lecture event featuring two journalists and the father of Courtney Love, all of whom believe Kurt Cobain was murdered. I visited the office of the Samaritans in London, England, the people who invented telephone distress counselling. In August 1997, I attended a funeral held by the daughter of a man who never got one after he committed suicide in 1956. I cruised the Net, regrettably and unwittingly witnessing a suicide in progress.

I seemed compelled to cover the waterfront, to ensure that suicide would never sneak up on me again, or that if it ever tried to, I would be better prepared. I made wonderful new friendships and became reacquainted with parts of myself that I had shut down long ago. I guess it's called playing the hand you are dealt. I would have infinitely preferred another, but as this was the one I got, I tried to enrich, rather than squander, the time I had to spend with it. Ignorance, I realized, is not bliss—it's only ignorance. I would far rather seek to know, even though that is at times painful.

Suicide may be as old as humanity, but so is storytelling, its role in restoring balance to a disrupted life long intuitively understood. "Tell the story. Bear witness. That's part of the healing," native elder Bea Shawanda of Sault Ste. Marie urged her audience in a powerfully eloquent speech delivered at a conference of the Canadian Association for Suicide Prevention in Toronto in 1996. In telling these painful stories, we pierce through individual isolation and acknowledge the people we loved and lost and continue to honour in our lives. In doing so, we strengthen ourselves and further our capacity to love, even when we have been massively wounded. As philosopher Sam Keen writes in his recent book, *To Love and Be Loved:*

The vigil that love keeps in the perennial darkness of human history does not give a vision of triumph or a promise of perfection. The great clarity it offers is the certain knowledge that we are sundered, dismembered, alienated from the totality to which we belong ("sinners," in old religious language)—and the hope . . . that what has been dismembered can be remembered . . . . To love . . . is to wager that communion rather than isolation is the ultimate fact that governs human destiny. . . .

The state of grief, especially after a traumatic loss such as suicide, has often been described metaphorically. I have seen it referred to as a "dark country" or a "private wilderness." After all my wandering, I found it to be a dark country in which there was eventually some light; a private wilderness that I stumbled through to a place of communion and remembering—a place as safe, and yet no doubt as precarious, as the place I fleetingly found sitting peacefully side by side with Daniel, one gentle evening a long time ago. I can live with that. I had faith then, a faith now restored, in the possibilities of life and love. I hope that in sharing this story, I can add to the dark country's light, help clear a path through the private wilderness for another weary traveller. I *hope.*

That is why I continue to live, and to write.

A CLOSED DOOR

WHEN I RECALL DETAILS OF THE DAY I found Daniel dead, as I have so many times in the five years since, I am tempted to detach myself, to watch the event unfold in my mind's eye without emotion, at the safe remove of time, in the light of selective memory, with the reputed benefit of hindsight and my capacity to fashion an interpretation that a reader might accept and understand. I can provide a version of events only. I am, after all, a flawed observer: biased, emotional, wounded, scarred, and at times still perplexed. There is so much I do not know, can never know. Daniel's suicide was a kind of ground zero in my life, and I must overcome the fear that if I poke around in the wreckage left in the wake of that devastation, I will find smouldering embers that still spark and burn. Yet this is something I must do, this clearing of dangerous debris, this making of a new, unobstructed pathway along which I may safely move forward.

To get to the centre of the experience, I have to start at its edges. What I see now is an emotionally stretched woman in her mid-thirties dancing as fast as she can around her boyfriend's depression. It's not as though depression itself is news to her. She's battled it herself and watched its insidious effects engulf others she's loved. She's no stranger to loss and grief, either, having survived a divorce and her mother's death from a stroke two years earlier. She has worked hard not to let her troubles swamp her entirely, and so far they haven't. She has seen enough human sadness and wasted spirit to know that not everyone lives happily ever after, and that she cannot simply expect it—happiness—to land in her lap, with no effort on her part.

But she doesn't always get it right. There's been therapy, enough to lay bare the obvious, all-too-common familial underpinnings of her own depression, and to show how this has—what else?— unconsciously predisposed her to choose similarly suffering souls as friends and lovers. Yes, she knows she's somehow programmed to be drawn to those who labour through difficult lives under the labels of "depressive," "addictive," "manic," and the like, to greater or lesser degrees. It's not hard to do anyway in creative circles, where artistic talent is often the saving grace of impoverished craziness—I use the term to encompass the spectrum, from garden-variety neurosis to more obvious manifestations of psychological pain and disorder.

And now there is Daniel, with whom she formed an intense and, for a time, happy relationship the previous year. They have reason to hope for good things, despite the difficulties Daniel is now having, emotionally and financially. She knows from hard experience that once depression has invaded and flourished, it takes time and care to prune it down from its threatening wildness to fit the garden of ordinary unhappiness. Still it can gain control in quick and frightening fashion, and it is almost impossible to ever weed out its deep roots entirely. She's kept it at bay for some time herself, and is determined to fight it off if it ever tries to take hold again.

Daniel too has been battling the infamous "black dogs" for years, with the aid of medications and regular visits to a psychiatrist he trusts. He talks openly about the help he gets and why he gets it. They have also talked about the shadow suicidal thoughts and feelings have cast on their lives in the past, and in Daniel's case, many years earlier, attempts. Their acceptance and compassion for each other are part of the strength of their relationship, or so it seems.

And though the depression may always be lurking, waiting for an opportunity to lunge, you would not know it, to view these two people pass the promising first months of their relationship. See them work, productively, at a variety of creative projects. Here they are striding up College Street, laughing and carrying on with friends. Here they are shopping and making meals together, collapsing on the living room floor at midnight during a heat wave, listening to each other's favourite music, discussing books, showing each other their work, sharing their most private dreams and desires. If there is an element of sadness in the mix, it isn't so hard to imagine, for those starting over with a new partner in their thirties are bound to feel the undertow of past failures. And that undertow is there all right. Along with the laughter and the light there are dark moments, when Daniel, recently separated, seems wracked by various guilts and regrets, and compelled to inform his new love, with extreme contrition, that he hasn't always behaved very nicely, especially back when he was a drunk. Sometimes, this need to confess and catalogue his sins strikes her as touching, incongruously innocent: "Listen," she wants to say, "if that's the extent of it . . . there's worse than you in this world, and they're not half so sorry!" Often, it seems, Daniel walks in the shadow of his own self-condemnation, and expects others to be no more compassionate toward him than a Texas parole board. Though redemption has been staring him in the face for some time, it seems sometimes he cannot see it, or imagine that it is real.

Remarkably, Daniel actually said at the beginning of their happy times that there was one thing he could promise her he would never do, not so long as they were together, and that was to kill himself. It never occurred to her that he might break such a startling and candid promise, never occurred to her that he might have had reason to. As far as she is concerned, she and Daniel are loyal allies in the war to survive the exigencies of a creative life in the hardbitten, downsized, fin-de-siécle world, with depressive illness thrown in as an added challenge, occasionally requiring the deployment of big emotional artillery. When it comes to these battles, she considers joint forces stronger than solitary troops.

After that declaration of Daniel's, suicide is not a part of their shared lexicon, not a spoken word that passes between them. But it seems in the end she didn't adequately perceive the degree to which her comrade had fallen and lost heart, or notice in time that his wounds had become life-threatening, that he'd decided to lie down and die, letting her run on—generously, he must have thought—sparing her the details of how badly off he really was. She always thought that one way or the other, they'd live to be hoary old veterans telling their war stories, stories Daniel had already begun to tell with such aching clarity in his poetry and fiction. The hope and optimism of their first summer together—how could she imagine it would be their last?—are a long way from the dead of winter to come.

Now I see myself in the early morning of that particular February day, walking down the two steep flights of stairs from Daniel's sprawling old apartment, with its rabbit's-warren layout and creaky hardwood floors, above a shoe store in a crumbling old brick building on College Street, in the middle of Toronto's now trendy "little Italy" neighbourhood. I set off to my small rented office farther east on College Street, where I do my work as a freelance magazine writer and editor. I am tired. I've been working hard, and Daniel has had the flu all week. With the physical symptoms of that to contend with on top of his other troubles, he is listless and sleeps fitfully, lying on the couch mostly, reading a little or watching TV. I feed him soup, keep him supplied with juice, throat lozenges, and Kleenex, cover him with blankets when they fall off while he dozes, run errands for both of us. Nurse Moira to the Rescue. Not a script I planned, or even knew I was following, but looking back, it appears I was quite a natural in my role among the ranks of failed saviours. As I now know, where there's a suicide, you'll often find us.

I see myself walking wearily up the street, wearing a black leather jacket, a black silk blouse, a black scarf splashed with a colourful floral pattern, the kind that hangs from racks by the dozens in the Latin American craft shops on Bloor Street between Bathurst and Spadina, and a pair of red denim jeans Daniel selected for me in a London boutique on my birthday the previous September. The colour red, a little alarming on a grey, sub-zero winter day in Toronto, is my one nod to Saint Valentine—I should mention shouldn't I, that it's Valentine's Day. This is something gossips would later make much of, attaching a bogus, romance-tinged melodrama to Daniel's exit from life on that day; his actual death was the night before.

But the reality is less florid. True, Daniel's personal life was rather a mess; he was separated, not divorced, from his wife, and our relationship was suffering from his ambivalence about this. I'd distanced myself a bit, maintaining a separate place to live, though I ended up spending more nights than not with him. I rationalized this as easier on both of us while he went through the inevitable inner conflicts of unravelling a difficult attachment. But I don't believe that this ordinary, if trying, human dilemma was linked in Daniel's mind with the pseudo-event of Valentine's Day. I think his deepening despair had by mid-February entered a kind of terminal phase that would have rendered the date irrelevant.

Earlier in the month, Daniel had come quietly into the living room, where I sat reading and drinking tea, and stood looking down at me with his best rather bashful smile. "Um, happy Valentine's Day," he said and presented me with one of those lottery tickets that lie in trays at the corner store, this one covered in shiny silver, pink, and red hearts. I laughed and thanked him for such a sweet, goofy gesture. "You're early," I said. "Isn't it the fourth?" he asked, startled. Yes, I replied, but Valentine's Day is the fourteenth. "Oh," he said. "I always seem to get those days mixed up."

Oh well. Daniel sat down beside me, and laughing at ourselves, a pair of writers living on the financial edge, we scratched off the hearts with a penny to see if we had won anything. Yes, we had. Two bucks. Wow. We never did get around to buying another ticket, and I have never had the heart to do so since. The unredeemed ticket sits in a box at the back of my closet, among other random mementoes I cannot seem to part with, but don't like to think about.

Still, whether intended as part of the story, a lividly ironic comment or not, Valentine's Day it was when I discovered Daniel dead, and I do live the day each year in the unavoidable glare of incongruous love-hype beaming in from all sides of the culture. The year following Daniel's death, I was working as an editor at *Equinox* magazine, then a Telemedia publication with offices in a glimmering glass high-rise building in North York. I debated whether to hide out at home that day, to brood, weep, light a candle, agonize, and isolate myself, but in the end felt I'd already done enough of that the previous year. So I went to work. I knew I would be meeting Lynn Crosbie for a quiet toast to Daniel that evening. Lynn, a fellow writer and neighbour, had forged a bond with Daniel over several years of mutual support for each other's creative efforts, and their shared battle with depression and agoraphobia. She too had been devastated by Daniel's suicide, and later wrote two poems, "Pearl," the title poem of her 1996 collection, and "Geography," in the same volume. Tender and horrific, they brilliantly captured Daniel's conflicted essence and the harrowing time of his death. Like several others in his life then, Lynn had recently had a falling out with Daniel, the kind of vague dust-up that often attends the writerly world of sensitive egos, and whose origins and meaning no one is really sure of in the end. But eternally unfinished business is one of the more burdensome realities of sudden death and, in particular, suicide. Lynn did not gloss over the tensions that had existed between her and Daniel at the time he died, but she had the grace to recognize them for the emotional ephemera they were (he mentioned her, with love, in his suicide note). She wrote of Daniel without damning judgment, and accorded her friend the dignity of forgiveness in death. I found it a comfort to know I would be with someone who understood that the better part of Daniel was a man to be deeply mourned, and missed. I looked forward to our meeting, and knew this would sustain me through the day.

Some time that morning, a mailroom clerk entered our office pushing a shopping cart filled with tiny white cardboard boxes tied up with red bows. "Any ladies here?" he called, sounding bored and a little embarrassed. The clerk wheeled the cart around to each woman's desk and plunked one of the boxes onto it. This was, it turned out, a tradition established by the company's president, and indeed, each box came with a typed-up, photocopied little tag with a Happy Valentine's Day wish from the boss.

We all laughed, the men suggesting they were going to file discrimination complaints but settling instead for a share of the ladies' chocolate-covered popcorn balls. Privately, I was glad I'd come to work and subjected myself to whatever Valentine crap might fly my way. A little box of sweets unceremoniously bestowed by the paid underling of a corporate executive I'd never met was about all I could handle anyway. It wasn't the first time, and wouldn't be the last, that outer and inner reality clashed wildly, in a way that demanded translation into comic irony. Grieving a suicide is like that, a constant tripping over cruel and abrupt juxta-positions between the tragic and the ridiculous. A year into the grieving process, I was beginning to get used to it, or so I comforted myself in believing.

But in the early afternoon of my own private D-day, one year earlier, I could never have imagined the turn my life was about to take, all the horrors that awaited. Now I flash back to the image of my oblivious, yet wary and anxious self walking back up the stairs in that dim hallway, my footfalls on the aluminum-trimmed linoleum steps echoing in my ears, the dry, acrid taste of fear gathering on my tongue. I reach Daniel's front door (a red door, as it happens, inviting the infamous coat of black), and turn the key in the lock, the words *he wouldn't* playing in my mind like a feverish mantra, their very presence unwelcome testimony that in some way, I actually think he would. I open the door with mustered determination, as though—I now tell myself wryly—a good attitude could have altered fate at that point. Christian miracles aside, I'm not one to believe that positive thinking can raise the dead.

But "dead" isn't what's on my mind in that moment. Now I tell myself everything is really okay, there is a rational and reasonable explanation for the morning's three unreturned phone calls. At worst Daniel is just in a deep sleep that has lasted into the early afternoon, after a restless night. I enter the apartment. The door to the living room is still closed, as it was more than twelve hours ago, when it seemed explainable. Daniel was sick, and the cat had disturbed him the night before, poking her paw in our faces and mewing to be fed at 5 a.m. He didn't want to keep me awake with his tossing and turning and coughing, so he told me he would sleep on the couch.

Yes, the closed door made sense then, but now my heart races and I somehow know I can no longer reasonably maintain the hope that everything is okay. I'm fending off the advent of deeper emotion by focusing on annoyance: *How dare you scare me this way? I will open the door, to hell with privacy, and say, "Daniel, what's going on?"* But when I turn the knob, the door won't budge. Locked. Another surge through my heart. I rattle the knob, pushing at the door and calling Daniel's name. Then I see the note. Tiny thing. A white piece of paper tacked on a white door. It says, in what is undeniably Daniel's hand, DO NOT COME IN. PLEASE CALL THE POLICE.

Later, I learned that the scant wording of this note supposedly echoed an event in a Martin Amis novel, but if Daniel had indeed intended to ornament the grim scene with a literary filigree, I'm afraid any such bookish allusion was lost on me then. Literarily speaking, the only thing I later at times wished was that I were possessed of the maniacally intrusive nature of one of Philip Roth's more memorable characters, namely Portnoy's mother, interminably haranguing her son every time he walks into the bathroom and shuts the door: "[Daniel], are you in pain? Do you want me to call the doctor? Are you in pain or aren't you? I want to know exactly where it hurts. Answer me." Yes, I have grimly thought to myself, if I were that kind of woman, perhaps I would have knocked sooner, knocked despite Daniel's telling me he needed an undisturbed night of sleep. I would have knocked and discovered the note much earlier, when there might have been time to save him, while he was still nodding into unconsciousness from the pills, before he had successfully affixed the plastic bags over his head and suffocated himself.

This is part of the futile and interminably self-punishing dialogue suicide survivors often have with themselves, the go-nowhere Dance of the Thousand If Onlys. For the other side of those musings is admitting that it is more likely (though not a certainty; I live with that painful truth) that Daniel was dead before I arrived back at the apartment the night before, after an evening's work toward a tight deadline at my office. The closed door did not signal danger to me then, and I did not knock or see the note. No, I was not a woman like Portnoy's mother. At that point in his life, Daniel was far more likely to choose the kind of woman who quietly respects privacy, who doesn't like to pry and prod, who would understand his needs, yadda, yadda, yadda, and who would consequently misread the final brick in a towering wall of despair as a perfectly understandable request for temporary sick leave. It has taken me years not to feel guilt about this; I do and always will feel regret. There is a profound and important difference.

In those awful first moments, however, I stand absorbing the note's message, stunned, my legs going weak. Now I am banging on the door, shoving myself against it, and shouting Daniel's name. When I stop for a moment to listen for an answer, a sound, anything, from the other side, there is only a terrible silence, settled and complete.

The mind's eye starts doing jump cuts here. I remember the next few hours only in a jerky, jumbled sequence. I know that once I had seen the note and it had registered that Daniel was not answering me, I ran to his office and dialed 911. Now I hear a strange sound issuing into the telephone receiver, a hysterical lady's voice, surely not mine, talking too rapidly of pills and a boyfriend and a locked door and *please send an ambulance now, right now.* Well, something like it, for I can't actually recall with any precision what I said.

Now, since I can do nothing about the locked door until help arrives, I am curiously driven to track through the apartment, roaming from room to room like some half-crazed zoo animal, with nothing to do but pace around the strange enclosure. What am I thinking? That Daniel is hiding under the discarded, claw-legged bathtub in a tiny back room used for storage? That he has somehow managed to squeeze himself in back of the refrigerator, or is planning to pop out from behind the bedroom door and say, "Fooled ya!"? I'm not thinking, just acting on dumb impulse. Yes, what I'd like is to make everything go back to "normal," anything, any explanation at all besides the one that is forcing its way into unwelcome being.

All I will let myself imagine in these moments is that Daniel has taken an overdose of medication, that he is unconscious, that as soon as the ambulance gets here, salvation and recovery will begin. That's it, an overdose, horrible enough, but right now, I am not thinking death, I will not allow death. "The heart did not believe," goes a line from Leonard Cohen's incantatory *Beautiful Losers,* and it is as accurate an expression of the human capacity to repel and deny loss as exists in the language. It's not so much a survival skill as it is an instinct, one that springs alert with particular strength in the face of abrupt, shocking death, wrapping us in a kind of protective psychological padding that dulls the impact of trauma.

So, no, I am still not thinking death, I am only thinking, and I believe saying aloud, things like *please hurry, please come, for Christ's sake get here, come now, please.* I don't know how long I waited, perhaps no more than five minutes, I don't think more than ten. Long enough to spin through the rooms, to shove myself against the door again, to shout Daniel's name and hear the awful silence, and finally, to fall to my knees on the patterned carpet in the hallway a few feet from the locked door, and the note that adorns it, feeling the word *NO* rising from my diaphragm, passing through my throat, and flinging itself hugely and forcefully from my mouth. As though *NO* could break down the door. As though *NO* could rip back time, sweep over the past, and reset its clockwork, so that it could resume ticking into the future minus this tragedy-in-progress. As though *NO* alone could go up against death itself and win.

Yet even though I am still fighting the possibility of death, a small part of me is getting the picture, and is now starting to bargain with God, or the gods, to think irrationally that perhaps a person can be a little bit dead, and can change his mind and crawl back to life, be scooped up and returned to the living, if he is not *too* dead, that is.

Finally, two bored-looking cops arrive, their black boots clumping up the stairs, the synthetic material of their massive blue winter coats incessantly swishing as they move. The older, bigger cop is dark-haired and blue-eyed; the other is blond and so young and fresh-looking that I almost want to apologize for exposing him to this.

I gesture to the door, and after they jiggle the knob and push against it themselves, they tell me to stand back, they're going to have to break it out of its frame. Shoulders to it, they heave their combined bulk just a couple of times, and I hear the oddly sickening sound of dry, old wood splintering, the wrenching give and groan of the heavy door falling inward and resting askew off its dislodged hinges.

Now that the door is open, the last thing I want to do, the last thing I am able to do, is enter that room. Shock has instilled in me a child's literal-mindedness: Daniel said in that note on the door not to come in, so I better not. Now that I am allowing for the possibility of death—death that can be bargained with, and reversed, mind you—I'm also starting to let myself form mental images of what scene might await. "He was capable of cruelty; he was meticulous, theatrical," writes Lynn Crosbie in her sad and beautiful poem for Daniel, "Geography." In it, she also writes of him as a "sweet friend," capable too of "rare, infectious bliss." But perhaps it is that cruel quality of Daniel's I recognize as I stand there, a quality that might have made him fashion some horrible tableau for the living to find. "An act like this is prepared within the silence of the heart, as is a great work of art," writes Camus of suicide in *The Myth of Sisyphus*. And what artful death, I could hardly have dared ask myself, had Daniel silently prepared?

It wasn't like that, in the end, but I suppose I had cause to fear Daniel's capacity for theatrics. He had told me of it himself and the memory of one such conversation stays with me. The previous summer, he and I had driven to Killarney to visit the family home of friends of mine, the prospect of "Jones camping" causing much hilarity in his circle. The general view was that the urban angst-man extraordinaire must be well and truly smitten to have agreed to let his Doc Martens tread on anything other than the concrete of a city sidewalk, to put himself beyond the orbit of the College Street *caffe latte,* even for a brief weekend. He did it happily, remarking on how strange it all was, how long it had been since he had placed himself in such a rugged environment, or done anything so outdoorsy as lounge on a wooden dock in a bathing suit, reading magazines. When he took a running dive and plunged into the cool lake, he popped up with a look of amazement on his face, and said, "I can't believe I did that. I don't know if I've ever done that," to the amusement of everyone else strewn lazily around the dock. It was like watching someone who usually lived within the squeeze of a vice-grip start to feel some loosening up, once again using muscles, emotional and physical, that have atrophied over a long time. Later, we spent an entertaining evening playing cards with my friend's good ol' boy brothers, who took to Daniel, even though it was obvious he aroused suspicions that he was a city guy of some airs and book learning. Besides, his drink of choice was diet Pepsi, not Molson Ex. During a round of euchre, one brother turned to another and called him a "bohemian, bag-bitin' whore." Daniel and I exchanged looks and laughed till we nearly fell off our chairs. We swore later that we would race each other to immortalize this wondrous colloquialism in a book; I guess I win.

On the way back, we drove along roads that channel like arteries through Muskoka's masses of billion-year-old granite. Daniel and I talked, as lovers getting to know each other do, of who we'd been before we'd met, long before, back even to the primordial ooze of high school. Amid the shared stories of teenage ineptitude and heartache was Daniel's description of himself as a budding young high-school playwright. He admitted one of the reasons he liked to write his own plays was because he could give all the good roles to himself. "Like what?" I wanted to know. He thought about it, and replied casually, "Oh, well, God."

Something about the way the word "God" hung in the air between us—the big kahuna of theatrical roles, none better!— evoked such naive adolescent audacity, a troubled boy's yearning for mastery of his world. It was so astonishing that we both began to chuckle. I pulled the car into a picnic area along the side of the road so I wouldn't lose control of the car as I was convulsed with laughter. Eventually we composed ourselves, and resumed our drive through miles of blasted-out Precambrian rock, back into the city, with its altogether different terra firma.

Daniel told me other stories that revealed his flair for drama, his desire to be at the centre of his own scenes, but that story, and the moment of its telling, in which he revealed so completely the innocent and all-too-human underpinnings of his self-aggrandiz-ing tendencies, often comes back to haunt me. "I love you, Moira, and I'm sorry, even though you will not imagine it," he wrote in his suicide note, only two seasons after our intimacy was at its promising beginning. *Oh, but I do imagine it, Daniel,* I have responded many times in dialogues I can't help having with his absence. *Unfortunately, I imagine it all too well, have endured much time in which about all I could do was imagine it, and that is the problem with this suicide of yours, Daniel, you see, the very big, heartbreaking problem.*

So, for reasons I could not have articulated at the time, two images crowd my mind as I stand paralyzed in the hallway by the broken door, suspended between not knowing and knowing what Daniel has actually done. Neither of them makes sense, couldn't occur simultaneously, much less if my chief image of Daniel unconscious on the couch is closer to reality. What I see is Daniel hanging dramatically, accusingly, somewhere in the room, perhaps from one of the towering and crowded shelves that hold his thousands of beloved books, or from the ceiling in the middle of the room, though this could not be, logistically or physically. I also see Daniel blown utterly apart, my mind making a metaphor of my deepest fear, that Daniel is now fragmented beyond reconstruction, forever gone, and that he himself has somehow enacted the horrible, unconscionable dismemberment.

That's what I see, the messy, terrible aftermath of a furious and violent act. What I feel is his rage, a rage encompassing the whole imperfect universe, and the chaotic heap of self that he so desper-ately sought to escape, when it seemed to have slipped out of his control. Mostly, I think, it is rage saved up, gathering gale force over years and years, and then turned inward, transformed into self-loathing and suicidal depression. "I thought I was trying to change, but I was not," is about the kindest thing Daniel says about himself in his final note, as he expresses the distorted notion that the only "right thing" for him to do is to remove himself from the planet entirely.

Young Cop and Older Cop do go into the room. I hear them murmuring, though I have no visual memory. Then, their boots clump to a standstill. A figure finally emerges from the room. Young Cop looks a little pasty as he looms before me. He is saying, "Why don't we go and sit down?" He is leading me away from the living room and into the kitchen. And I'm thinking, *Okay, so I don't have to go into that room, I don't ever have to see whatever sorry spectacle has unfolded there. I don't want to see Daniel in this undignified and horrible state of self-inflicted death. If he'd wanted me to see that, would he not have left the door unlocked? Would he have left the note explicitly warning whoever found it—and he had to know the person was going to be me—not to come in?*

I never do go into the room; I only catch a glimpse of Daniel's resting body as I leave the apartment, as the ambulance attendants and cops prepare to navigate the steep and narrow staircase with their grim cargo of a six-foot-one, 200-pound, thirty-four-year-old dead man. I feel no desire to behold this. The man I knew and loved is gone. Absurdly, I am not in a position to identify his body officially anyway, not being his "next of kin." That joyous job fell to his wife.

My memory of the last time I saw Daniel remains less violent, though it speaks of what was to come in a way I didn't understand at the time. The day had been good, companionable, quiet. Daniel stood in the hallway as I was preparing to leave for an evening of work at my office, saying he was not feeling well again. He went into the living room and lay down on the couch. Before I left, I sat down beside him as he faced inward, put my hand on his shoulder and asked if he was going to be okay. He nodded a little. Anything he needed while I was out? He shook his head. I kissed him on the cheek and said, "I'll see you later." As I recall, he did not respond. If the time he cites in his suicide note is correct, a little more than an hour after I left, he swallowed his overdose and began preparing to suffocate himself with plastic bags—a method that comes courtesy of the popular recipe book *Final Exit.* Dr. Sherwin Nuland describes the method in his illuminating study of modern death, *How We Die,* as about the most painless and humane way there is to go.

As we settle at the table and the young officer pulls out his notebook, I'm asking, in what must seem a spaced-out way, "Is he dead?" Somehow, he of the fresh face and stammering tongue manages not to answer that question directly. I am given a further reprieve from the truth, though of course, I know by now it is true, has to be. Why would everything be so very strange if Daniel were not dead?

I'm asked if I'd like a glass of water. Everything is happening very slowly now, as though we're immersed in something viscous, something jelling and holding us. Water? A glass of it? Are you going to get it for me? Why would you offer me a glass of water? I strain to understand, as though grasping the precise meaning of this question might somehow explain what is going on in the other room.

More cops arrive, and ambulance attendants. Soon the apartment is crawling with large men murmuring in deep, urgent voices. In the end, it is a burly, deadpan, sandy-haired paramedic entering the kitchen wearing latex gloves who tells me that Daniel is dead. What he actually says is couched in some kind of official-speak about there appearing to be "no signs of life," that the coroner would have to confirm that and he'd be arriving shortly. Only at this point do I cry, though not yet in full-out sobs. I am after all a Wasp by training and upbringing. Loss of control will come later, alone.

For now, I sit like a good girl on my chair in the kitchen, feeling small and immobilized while the big men do their job. From where I sit, I see a blur of human traffic in the hallway, legs in dark pants, feet in boots, moving back and forth, clump, clump, clump. I fix on two objects on the carpet there. What are they, anyway? My jacket, curled and twisted in a heap, the arms inside out. I must have squirmed out of it and let it drop to the floor at some point. There's my scarf in a pile nearby too. I watch, numbly fascinated, as the succession of legs and feet step over these things, until one cop notices them and picks them up, straightening out the jacket and hanging it and the scarf on the back of a kitchen chair. It's the same officer who makes *shhhh* noises and rushes to close the kitchen door, seeing me put my hands over my ears as another cop in the hallway starts reading Daniel's suicide note out loud in a mocking tone to the assembled masses of post-mort officialdom. I sit, listening in speechless horror.

At some point, Young Cop escorts me to the phone in Daniel's office, so that I may call a friend. But which friend? My mind is so addled, I cannot remember a single phone number. I sit for a while in this different chair, Daniel's chair, occasionally picking up the receiver and again, like a child imitating the movements of the adult world, press the numbered keys in what might be, but isn't, a familiar sequence. Young Cop hovers awkwardly behind me, asking if I have an address book and could he get it for me? Well, yes, I have one, but it's at my office, I explain.

It's mortifying. I finally remember that one of the women I share a house with, Jeannie, will be at the Ryerson School of Journalism today, and of all the numbers that dwell in my head, this institution's is the one I recall. An alarmed secretary—I guess I sound pretty bad—finds my friend and soon she is on her way over in a cab. The officers seem more able to talk with her than with me, for I recall bits of information being relayed to me through her as an intermediary. Older Cop—he who read Daniel's last written words out loud—enters the kitchen and, apparently trying to offer some condolences, stands beside me and says, "Ya know, Myra—is that how you pronounce your name?—if he was that far gone that he was capable of doing something like this, you're better off without him. With sick people like that, if it isn't this year, it's gonna be next, and there's really not much you can do about it."

So, Older Cop becomes the first in what was to be a long line of people to offer me pat truisms and pet theories about suicide, none of them useful to someone in the first stages of coming to terms with the actual suicide of a real human being she knew and loved. Yet training in handling suicides does exist for police officers; considering how woefully common it is for the police to deal with these situations—not least within their own ranks—it is difficult to understand why an officer at a downtown precinct of a metropolis with a population of millions would not know better. The last thing I hear, as I am being led down the stairs, I think by Jeannie and the one woman officer in the place, is Older Cop once again reading aloud from Daniel's note, and a snippet of the conversation of two other cops, who are standing in what had been the bedroom. "Great apartment, eh?" says one. "Yeah," replies the other. "Guy sure had a lot of books."

At my office a few blocks down the street, I compose myself and phone several people I think should know what has happened. I seem to need to say it to believe it. I transmit the information, I hear the stricken voices respond, I don't recall what was said to whom exactly. *I'm afraid I have bad news. Daniel killed himself, yes, that's right, yes, yes.* In the middle of my grim task, an editor calls from *Flare* magazine, which has just published a story of mine. A local radio station wants to interview me later in the week, and the editor reminds me that in such interviews I should use the name of the magazine as much as possible, as in, "Well, Bob, as I wrote in *Flare*...." "Okay, sure, no problem," I reply. "Happy Valentine's Day," she says with a small giggle as she signs off. "Same to you," I say as I hang up.

The woman officer knocks on the door. I gather some belongings, feeling dizzy, unreal. I follow her silently down the wide, sweeping staircase of this old building that was once an Orange Lodge in Toronto's good Protestant Irish days, one my paternal grandfather probably belonged to, and which by 1994 was housing an alternative cinema, as well as the offices of various writers and artists. Jeannie is in the front seat of the cruiser, holding my bug-eyed cat in her arms. The cat, as opposed to Daniel, had wedged herself under the old bathtub, and must have cowered there all afternoon.

I sit in the cruiser's back seat, shiny and worn from the all the backsides that have graced it before mine, separated from those in the front by a wall of wire caging. I am surely one of the more docile passengers the car has transported. I stare through the window, up into the sky, beyond the tops of passing houses.

Is there something primal, universally human, in this intense urge to gaze toward the heavens after a death? The night my mother died, I sat outside in the October chill, compelled to watch the sky as dawn came, sure I saw her face in the wisps of cloud, moving slowly, grandly, through all the unique expressions of hers that are imprinted on my memory, passing overhead, dissolving, disappearing. Do we really imagine our loved ones have gone up there? Do we truly expect to see them waving good-bye to us, smiling, telling us they are going to be fine now? All I know is that I can't seem to stop myself staring up at the whitish-grey, late-afternoon sky, enlivened only by the stark contrast of dark, bare-branched trees, a matte winter canvas on which to rest my battered senses, as the cruiser ferries us home. No, no signs of Daniel up in that frozen, empty sky.

My other roommate, Grainne, has returned from work early, having heard the news from Jeannie. She is standing in the living room when we come through the door. Seeing the look of genuine pain on her face, I suddenly, momentarily, understand how this death is going to affect the people surrounding him, even those who are closer to me than to him; yes, suicide kills everyone, as the English essayist G. K. Chesterton astutely observed before his suicide. Grainne rushes to put her arms around me. We stand together like that for a long time.

Later in the evening, several other close friends come to the house, and we sit in the living room for hours, long into the night, as the phone rings and I must speak again and again to the growing circle of people who now know of Daniel's death. We veer from deep and dreadful discussions of this thing that has happened, the reason that we're all gathered here so abruptly, and lighter conversation that keeps everyone connected to the world beyond this tragedy. I sit in my chair in the corner of the room, nursing an Irish whisky someone has thoughtfully placed in my hand as I return once again from the phone and listen dazed as the people around me engage in an exchange about canoeing. *Well,* I am thinking, my head fuzzy from the combination of shock and alcohol, as I'm hit by a bizarre urge to laugh hysterically, *Daniel is dead, and what better time to plan next summer's excursion to Quetico Park?* It makes no sense, but nothing does. I can suggest no other subject that would be more suitable for a roomful of people who don't all know each other well, though they know me. Etiquette books say nothing about how to behave in the wake of a death by suicide, though Hallmark has recently designed a greeting card to send to someone grieving a suicide, with distinctly religious overtones. My friends' gentle, intermittent attempts that evening to socialize politely in the midst of accepting the enormity of the loss at hand were touchingly human. It won't be the last time that this sense of high absurdity will strike me in my struggle to accept Daniel's death and its many sad consequences.

By two in the morning, everyone had either gone to bed or left, except the heroic Laima, whom I have known since I was a nervous nineteen-year-old at the University of Toronto. She had arrived earlier in the evening with her husband, Larry, both of them rather gussied up, which I didn't understand until later, when I remembered that it was Valentine's Day. My call had come just as they were heading out the door to enjoy a romantic dinner; instead of a relaxed, uninterrupted evening of candlelight and wine, they got suicide and canoeing in my living room. But I'm not aware of that right now, at 2 a.m. I say to Laima, "I just don't think I can go to bed. I don't think I can stand any darkness." She insists I lie down on the couch and at least rest. Hands folded in her lap, her dark skirt flared around her, like some nursing sister of mercy keeping vigil in the flickering candlelight at the bedside of a wounded soldier, my beloved friend says she will sit by me until I do fall asleep. Finally, after a fitful half hour or so, I pretend that I am taking the longer, deeper breaths of sleep, so that she can go home and get some herself. She tiptoes out and quietly shuts the front door. I reluctantly, painfully, drag myself upstairs to my own bed.

All through the night, Daniel is with me, trying to struggle back from death; or is it all me, still trying to rescue him? He hovers in the howling February night outside my window, tapping on the glass, a Heathcliff blown in from the moors. I pull him through and try to still his shivering, to warm his near-frozen limbs. He hangs in my closet, and just in time I cut the lethal knot. He falls to the floor, red-faced and coughing, living and breathing nonetheless. He calls to me from the bottom of a dark well, and somehow I find the strength to pull him up from the echoing depths. He is washed ashore on tumultuous, crashing waves, pulled back into the roaring black water by a taunting and relentless undertow; still, I grasp his hand and drag him to the safety of the windswept beach.

In all of these visions, I imagine someone who does not, who cannot, wish to die. It was a mistake, surely. Can't a person change his mind? Even when my thoughts aren't involuntarily racing to produce an image or metaphor to shoulder my pain and fear, I feel Daniel surrounding me—this was the man I'd slept with the night before last, the night before his last night alive, the man who held me in his arms and said, "I love you *so much,*" in a tone that I will never forget, and that I now understand meant that he was saying goodbye to me. Lying there helplessly, I have what strikes me now as the most pitiable bout of magical thinking: *If Daniel were alive, he would be so sorry for the grief he has caused. He would wish he hadn't done this. He would want to take it all back.*

These strange feelings carry me through the night, and are the first in a long series of visions, dreams, and nightmares that I will have as I struggle to fill Daniel's absence with memories and fantasies of his presence. These images are not comforting: Daniel in prison, meeting me in the visitors' area, clearly having been beaten. There is no escape, and so little I can do for him: Daniel in some hellish psychiatric institution, where he has been lobotomized and fundamentally changed, no longer himself; Daniel kidnapped and brainwashed by evil forces, locked away in a strange house, where I can't find the way back out. Or, and this was a recurring and barely conscious hope that I admit with some embarrassment, Daniel is just away, gone to a far-off land; like some long-lost sailor in a classic folk tale he will one day appear on my doorstep, older and wiser, more weathered, altered, still recognizably himself, and filled with stories of pain and glory I am only too eager to hear, as we sip our tea, warm and safe, reunited by the fireside.

Yes, Daniel is many things in these visions, dreams, and nightmares, but the one thing he is not is dead. It will be four years before I have my one and only dream of Daniel in which he is not threatened or horribly changed or in some kind of danger. When I wake from it, I recognize that it was a dream in which Daniel at last appeared to me as he once was, not as I fear or wish he was, and that I had dreamed of him as I might have dreamed of anyone else in my life, without horror.

But it's only my waking, rational self that understands what his absence means in the beginning of this process of letting go. And on the night after his death, this rational self is utterly swept away by deep pain and emotion.

I couldn't have known, as I rose reluctantly to face the day that followed, that in this shattered state, I was about to embark on a long, arduous journey of mourning that I had no choice but to make.

The work of grief had only begun.

DANIEL,
WE HARDLY KNEW YOU

AS THE MONTHS AND YEARS HAVE PASSED since
Daniel's death, I have often looked back on those final days and
wondered how it was that I never translated my inchoate fears of
what might happen into the dreaded word "suicide." At worst, I
thought that if Daniel's depressed mood continued to spiral down-
ward, it would render him helpless to cope with living alone in his
apartment and he would have to stay with me, or someone else
who could help him recover. The most grim thought of all, I
wondered if he would have to be hospitalized. That seemed like
rock bottom, and I was prepared to do what I could to make sure
Daniel didn't hit it. I knew that his greatest fear was of a return to
the severe terrors of agoraphobia he had experienced years earlier,
when he was trying to conquer alcoholism. As he saw it, the drinking had merely masked the depression and phobia he had begun
to suffer in his early teens, and that had laid in wait to pounce on
him as he struggled to become sober.

The young American novelist Andrew Solomon, writing in *The
New Yorker* in 1997, brilliantly described his harrowing bouts of
depression at its most extreme—so paralyzing that he spent days
in bed, lying in his own urine, rather than face the terror of even

simple movement—in words that hauntingly echoed for me Daniel's own graphic accounts of the affliction. So far, Solomon remains alive, with the aid of medications, supportive friends, an extraordinarily nurturing father who literally spoon-fed and washed his thirty-one-year-old son when he could not do it himself, and an admirable, unsentimental desire to affirm the value of life. Still, he heard what he calls the "seductress" of the suicidal impulse in his darkest times, knows others who have surrendered to it, and does not smugly suggest the siren call could never tempt him again.

Yes, that's how bad it gets for some. And even then, survival is possible. Yet Daniel viewed the prospect of another round of alcohol abuse followed by the hellish symptoms of withdrawal as unendurable: "I'd rather chop my head off than go through that again," he once told me dryly, as we sipped coffee on the outdoor patio of the Cafe Diplomatico one balmy day in June. He had explored some of the more horrifying aspects of that nightmare in his novel *Obsessions*. At the time, he seemed determined to never again find himself in such darkness.

Now, I know that given Daniel's set of "risk factors," and the place he would come to occupy as a statistic, he was practically a textbook case of a suicide waiting to happen: a young white male with a history of depression, alcoholism (though sober for eight years), previous suicide attempts, with a recent marital split and financial difficulties. These latter problems he sought to solve by doing something else that is a telltale sign of suicidality: getting rid of possessions, in his case, an impressive collection of modern first-edition books. There were also strained relations and outright estrangement from some family members and friends, and a string of disappointments concerning his work. Of course, if Daniel was in one of the highest risk groups for suicide, it occurred to me later that I, as someone predisposed to fall in love with a young man of this description, by virtue of my own age and sex and more personal identifying markers, had also entered a high-risk group, statistically speaking—the league of women demographically poised to mourn the suicides of these men.

There are statistics, diagnoses, categories and risk factors, trends and theories, and then there are real people and their unique lives. It seems that many still lack a language with which to adequately express, even to themselves, the nameless, formless despair that feeds on itself and grows bigger and more dangerous, more self-destructive. We speak now commonly of "depression," though it is, as author William Styron writes in *Darkness Visible* of his own frightening bout of it, "a noun with a bland tonality and lacking any magisterial presence, used indifferently to describe an economic decline or a rut in the ground, a true wimp of a word." Forsaking any sense that profound feelings of sadness might have a spiritual dimension, a greater purpose, if only to alert us that something is very wrong internally and externally with our lives, with our whole beings, we seem to expect people armed with medical degrees and pharmaceutical compendiums—wisdom and compassion optional—to take away our pain, solve our problems, make us better with a scrawl on a prescription pad. But any under-standing of depression (for lack of a better word) that reduces it to its organic causes and effects alone, and the people suffering from it to mere biological entities with lists of symptoms to be treated, is an impoverished one.

By all indications, however, suicide was always a possibility for Daniel. "It's like all the trains came into the station at once, and there just weren't enough tracks," mused a friend shortly after Daniel's death. The expanding freight of misfortunes culminated in what suicide experts refer to as a "triggering event." In Daniel's case, it was the news in early February that publication of his book of short stories scheduled in a matter of weeks—advance manuscripts of the work had been sent out to the media for review, and he was to read at Toronto's Harbourfront reading series in March—had been delayed indefinitely. It was a situation fraught with acrimony and complications that did not die with Daniel, and which it must be said he played a part in creating, as he followed what appears to be in hindsight a relentless course of escalating self-sabotage. As is clear from his suicide note, it felt to him like a final, stunning failure, one that he did not believe he had the strength to redeem.

Yes, I look at all this today and can practically see a large movie marquee blinking brightly in the darkness above Daniel's apartment, announcing:

VALENTINE'S DAY SPECIAL!
ONE NIGHT ONLY!
THE SUICIDE OF DANIEL JONES
STARRING DANIEL JONES

(This followed by, in much smaller letters, somewhere near the bottom: *and Moira Farr as the girlfriend—who didn't know*).

In the context of statistics and risk factors I learned about after the fact, it seems odd that Daniel's suicide would shock anyone who knew him. Yet despite the risk profile he theoretically embodied, or the fact that his writing had always been rife with references to suicide—indeed, took the reader all too closely into the troubled mechanics of the suicidal mind—no flashing sign proclaimed the imminent event. During his final days, Daniel did and said things and behaved in ways that he must have intended to throw me and others off the suicidal scent. Again, this is a not uncommon pattern for suicidal people. Time after time, survivors report with heartbreaking irony that if anything, the depressed people they have lost seemed in better spirits than usual in the days leading up to their suicides.

Those who study suicide say that the energy required to carry one out usually comes only when the person's depression has lifted somewhat. What family and friends think with relief is a positive uplift in mood may only reflect the person's own relief that he or she will soon be dead, and therefore no longer burdened with intolerable pain—or "psychache," a term coined by Edwin Shneidman, the psychologist considered the founder of the field of suicidology. And so, all kinds of clues that seem so obvious once the person is gone add up to something quite different while he or she is still alive and functioning, doing it better than has been the case for some time.

And maybe that is true. In one of the most painfully resonant observations I have read on the subject, Alfred Alvarez writes in *The Savage God:* "A suicidal depression is a kind of spiritual winter, frozen, sterile, unmoving. The richer, softer and more delectable nature becomes, the deeper the internal winter seems, and the wider and more intolerable the abyss which separates the inner world from the outer." I felt a terrible sadness when I first read these words, for their implied interpretation of all the changes Daniel tried to make in the last year of his life. Perhaps his embarking on a new romantic relationship was partly a desperate effort to allay the deep depression that always threatened to terrorize him. Once the first glow of the romance began to dim a little, I wonder, did he feel a huge sense of disappointment and even fear? Did he ever articulate the thought to himself that even grand feelings of love weren't going to chase away his black dogs for good? Was this experience the painful backdrop for his unfolding suicidal plan? It hurts to think so, and for a time after his death, brooding on this fuelled much of my sadness and self-pity. Like the bumbling loser protagonist of E. Annie Proulx's novel *The Shipping News,* I flagellated myself with a series of incriminating headlines bannering my brain:

STUPID WOMAN WANTS TO SETTLE DOWN
AND LIVE HAPPY LIFE, FALLS FOR DEPRESSED
WRITER

STUPID WOMAN FAILS TO SAVE SUICIDAL
BOYFRIEND

SAVE SELF, FRIENDS, EXPERTS URGE STUPID
WOMAN

For a time, I regarded with disgust a world that skips merrily along on unexamined romantic fantasies that love conquers all, love is all you need, love lifts us up where we belong, any kind of love is better than no love at all, and so on. I had so wanted to believe it. Daniel and I loved each other, no question of that. But, contrary to the pop propaganda, love wasn't enough to obliterate despair, saved no one, did not mean never having to say you're sorry, failed to lift us higher and higher, or coax us into believing that with this love of ours, which had no beginning and had no end, we could make everything all right. I endured an unpleasant period when I privately and bitterly seethed at those who believed that love had gotten them or someone they cared for through a tough situation. I envied them their unsullied faith in their own human powers, their sunny belief in a mellow and benevolent God who, when not restoring fallen baby sparrows to their nests, spends his time making everything nice for special little them. I viewed with contempt their ability to embrace an expansive sense of love's capabilities, at a time when mine had been thoroughly destroyed. If there were a Heartbreak Olympics, I figured I deserved gold, and for a time, all I wanted to do was to rest on my dubious, self-awarded laurels.

This kind of bitterness is not uncommon among the mourning and the traumatized. Any illusion that you have control over your life or that of another has been viciously ripped away. Suddenly, you are cast out from the world of unravaged souls able to trust their own good emotional navigation, their own personal goodness, while you limp along, hopelessly flawed, a pariah, uninvited to the celebration of happiness you imagine everyone else is enjoying. If anything spurred me to get serious about facing the grief, it was my shamed feeling that I couldn't genuinely extend good wishes for happiness to others.

Owning up to the fact that I was wasting a lot of time and energy feeling sorry for myself was humbling. "The world breaks everyone, and afterward some are strong at the broken places," wrote Ernest

Hemingway in *A Farewell to Arms*. Perhaps his own eventual suicide indicates he did not include himself in the strong "some." But it seems appropriate that a 1990 book heralding the new and widening focus on human "resilience," as opposed to dysfunction, in social work and psychotherapy, takes its title from this bit of Hemingway. The book's author, Linda T. Sanford, a Boston psychotherapist, interviewed people who had overcome extreme abuse and loss in childhood, many of whom had chosen work in helping professions. Some expressed dismay that their lives had been marked so severely by trauma, and wondered if they might have been different people, making different choices, if they had not had their bad experiences. But they were people who succeeded in spite of—indeed, because of—their wounds, people who tried to use their understanding and knowledge positively, genuinely believing they were wiser counsellors to the bereaved and traumatized owing to their own experiences. They could help others more effectively, since they could truly empathize with their pain; in this sense, something good had arisen from their own difficulties, something they came to accept and value on its own painfully born terms.

Healing, to be real and complete, doesn't mean that scars reminding you of severe past wounds disappear. It can and should mean a restoration of one's faith in the enduring possibilities of life and love: your life, your love. Tolstoy recognized this when he wrote, "Only people who are capable of loving strongly can also suffer great sorrow, but this same necessity of loving serves to counteract their grief and heals them." The wise novelist's words appear on the introductory pages of a well-regarded handbook for grief counsellors.

And so, though it stings to imagine it, for I naively assumed that the support and love I offered Daniel might at least offset some of his depression, I now wonder if he was playing some horrific game of chicken with himself in those final days. It is hard to read his suicide note's careful accounting of what he finally decided to do and why, hard not to turn away from the unforgiving glare of the words he wrote in a trembling script, less than two hours after our last goodbye:

> between 6:45 and 7:00 took approx. 45-50 Ativan (1 mg.)
> . . . shaking all over, but fully conscious . . . I would liked to be nearly passed out before closing the bag(s) completely around my neck with the rubber bands. Will this happen? I have handcuffs, to cuff myself in a position where I am incapable of tearing the bags . . . should I have to suffocate myself in full consciousness . . . I will go through with it, but it seems extremely unpleasant . . . I have long wanted to do it, but fear alone has prevented me.

I knew he was despondent over yet another rejected writing-grant application the previous week. He did not mention the postponed book to me, which he would have known about several days earlier. Yet he refers to it in his lengthy suicide note and, as though helpfully laying out evidence, he neatly compiled the terse, rejecting correspondence that must have stung so harshly in a prominent place on his desk. Lots of conflicting clues indicate now that he was enduring a kind of ambivalence towards life that is common among suicidal people, seesawing between "I will/I can't" almost until his final hour.

Evidence suggests that the suicidal state is indeed hellishly Janus-faced. American journalist George Howe Colt, in his 1991 book, *The Enigma of Suicide*, cites many examples of people who, after surviving serious suicide attempts, express relief that they failed, and gratitude that their lives were saved—lives which, up to the very moment of their self-destructive actions, they apparently did not wish to continue. In one extraordinary instance, a man who survived a jump from San Francisco's Golden Gate Bridge (often referred to as the suicide capital of the world, though now fenced to prevent jumps, and routinely patrolled and monitored for would-be jumpers), explains how the moment he leapt off and was airborne, he understood with horror that he had made a mistake and suddenly felt a frantic desire not to die. Accounts such as these do nothing to comfort the loved ones of successful suicides, who may prefer to think that the deceased did not feel anything in the moments before dying or they were so sure of their course, they at least got their wish, and are no longer suffering. Painful though it may be to face, it is more likely that this is not so. It is standard now in the treatment and study of the suicidal to assume ambivalence, on one side of which is indeed a desire to live.

Those of us close to Daniel, and there weren't many at that point, hadn't been given enough overt reason to look seriously at how desperate he had become in so short a time. I had thought about calling his psychiatrist or one of his friends to confide my worries but didn't, considering that meddlesome. Daniel's psychiatrist, whom he liked and trusted, and had visited regularly for eight years, was stunned by the news of his death, and pored over his session notes from the previous weeks and months, vainly searching for decisive signs of Daniel's shift into crisis that he might have missed.

Even Daniel's efforts to divest himself of possessions and previous attachments, in one regard a classic precursor to suicide, could also be interpreted as healthy emotional housecleaning that he felt was overdue. Daniel had a rueful self-awarenes of the obsessive-compulsive underpinnings of his book collecting. While visiting my sister in London, England, the previous summer, we had stopped at a curio shop window in which were displayed an array of T-shirts adorned with witty cartoons and captions. One showed a nerdish fellow with a serious expression sitting at a table on which were spread small round objects. The caption underneath said, "Fred was upset to find a Rice Krispie in his Corn Flake collection." Daniel burst into a loud cackle of appreciation at this, tears forming at the corners of his eyes as we wended our way home. "I'm laughing because it's true! It's sick, that's how bad it is, this collecting business." (The next day, my sister went to buy the shirt for Daniel. It had already been sold; the problem is clearly endemic. Instead, she bought us each a T-shirt printed with the clean, green-and-white cover graphics of the original Penguin paperbacks — *The Thin Man* for Daniel, and *Farewell, My Lovely* for me. It was one of the first things I gave away after his death.)

And so, by Daniel's own account, the hobby that gave him pleasure could also be a burden, just one more thing for the mind to find fault with and patrol for disorder to a picayune degree. On one occasion, Daniel returned from a bookstore foray with a remaindered novel by William T. Vollman, which had been listed in a collectors' magazine as potentially valuable. Daniel had laughed as he showed it to me: "You see, I didn't buy it because I want to read it. I have no idea why it's considered valuable. But it was there, so I had to get it."

On another occasion, I was perusing Daniel's shelves and sat down on a box, one of many that littered the room, as he sorted through and put aside things he wanted to get rid of after he separated from his wife. "You're sitting on my *Tamarack Reviews*," he said, hovering behind me. I looked up, not sure what he meant. "It's a complete set. There may only be one other one in Canada." I stood, and Daniel, looking grave, took the box and placed it off in a corner, out of danger of being sat upon again. I couldn't help teasing him a little afterwards. "How about I sit on your *Tamarack Reviews*?" I would say, when he seemed unnecessarily bothered by some minor matter.

Daniel's obsessive-compulsive side also found expression in day-to-day routines. Unlike other men I'd encountered, Daniel was competent domestically, perhaps overly so, with a need to be surrounded by clean countertops and very organized shelves. Order comforted him, and his urge to stave off anxieties in this way was far greater than my own. My more laissez-faire style must have troubled him on some subconscious level. I had to smile at such times, as when, after I'd loaded a washing machine at the local laundry and slung the large canvas bag loosely onto a table, Daniel reflexively picked it up and folded it neatly.

Daniel himself was all too aware of the negative side of this compulsive obsessing over matters that pass almost unexamined through less fretful minds. There were occasions when he would explain some complicated situation to me, why he couldn't do this or that, the double, or quadruple edges of some decision that had to be made, the mutually exclusive options that were not options at all, the endless looping spirals of detail painstakingly discerned and teased out and closely regarded. Sometimes I felt I'd lost the thread of the thing entirely and wanted to scream in frustration. Daniel was expert at fashioning existential knots around himself, the kind that only tighten further each time you try to loosen and move free of them, while I stood on the outside wondering impatiently why they couldn't just be cut away altogether.

No, life was not simple for Daniel, and he lamented that himself, especially when it came to literary business. "I feel like I'm from the eighteenth century," he once commented with dismay, as he groused about some linguistic offence committed in print that he wished to protest formally in a letter. He feared he'd be made to feel foolish by people who either hadn't noticed or didn't care. He was punctilious about his own writing and editing, and could be savage about others' mistakes or sins of sloppiness.

If details threatened to swamp him, a larger part of Daniel's love of books and language was far from onerous. "I was aware of the delight that reading and purchasing books held for him. I was not, however, aware of his total passion for collecting until seeing his complete library," wrote a Toronto book dealer, Janet Fetherling, in a catalogue she compiled of Daniel's collection, which she bought after his death. "Here was someone who put his dust-jacket covers on with a folding-bone, owned specialised bibliographical reference material, and possessed a computer program for his records. Considering everything else he did, I don't see how he found the time." Daniel also found time to search out and read largely unknown works published by small Canadian literary presses. After his death, more than one writer remarked to me how pleasantly taken aback he or she had been to be approached by Daniel after publishing something in a chapbook or small-press edition, and how appreciative of his thoughtful comments and words of encouragement. The Canadian literary world can be a dispiriting place, where obscurity until awards have been won is the norm, sour grapes are a dietary staple, and praise where it is due a rarity. In this withering atmosphere, Daniel knew how much a small gesture could mean to a struggling writer. As he sorted through his books, he gave several to me that he thought I might like. The last one of these was *The Lover of Horses,* by Tess Gallagher, partner of the late American short-story writer and recovered alcoholic Raymond Carver, and herself a writer whom Daniel admired.

Even selling books could give him deep satisfaction. "Daniel enjoyed the disposal of books as well as the acquisition of them," Fetherling also observed in her catalogue. "I'm sure I'll buy more, and have just as big a collection sooner or later," Daniel told me wryly, as he prepared for the grand clearance. It didn't occur to me to confront him and say, "You're not selling these because you plan to kill yourself, are you?" Especially in the beginning of our courtship, this sorting and selling seemed something he wanted to do, a symbolic starting over, and I didn't question it.

Daniel had, after all, endured so much through his painful young years, and with immense effort, had survived serious depression, phobias, and the terrible places, both physical and emotional, that his alcoholism had taken him—alcoholism that functioned as a mask and a distraction from those other disorders. As is the case with hardcore addicts, once Daniel stopped drinking, he faced the real work of dealing with his fears and emotional problems. With much help from others that he acknowledged, he did that work, and had made his way. Without consulting a suicide risk–assessment checklist, there would have been no reason in the minds of his friends and colleagues to bring in the commital forms. Daniel would have vehemently rejected them anyway. In earlier poems and stories, he had captured the unique pathos of living in a mental ward. Daniel would have viewed a return there as a disastrous defeat and step backwards; for so long, he had moved himself away from that world, from that possibility.

When suicides happen, especially when we feel in hindsight that we failed to see what we should have seen, we must forgive ourselves. Demographers and various medical experts aside, we don't generally view the people we love as micro-data units under the cold light of a larger statistical checklist of telltale signs, or assess them with clinical detachment ("I'm sorry, Daniel, but after consulting the *Diagnostic and Statistical Manual of Mental Disorders,* I've reached the conclusion that you are at a high risk for suicide. Get help, and goodbye"). Would the suicide rate be much affected if we did this? It's absurd to seriously imagine so on a sociological level, but naturally I have asked myself whether knowing what I know now, I might have responded differently to Daniel as he slipped further into his lonely decision.

Forming a relationship with Daniel's parents, in particular his mother, was one of the many unexpected things that happened after Daniel's death. Our bond was a painful one, but it was also healing in unforeseen and subtle ways. I can say with some certainty that this relationship would not have unfolded if Daniel had not died. In such strange twists does suicide throw a wild card into the deck you thought you knew well enough to predict, drawing you off in startling directions, challenging you to play an unfamiliar new hand.

Daniel had been estranged from his father for many years; there was only a handful of contacts between them after Daniel left home for university. Nor did his sister keep in touch with Daniel; I met her only once, at his funeral. Daniel was not comfortable visiting his parents' home, and maintained a connection only with his mother, who met with him occasionally when she visited Toronto. Clearly, the reasons for this estrangement were a source of great pain to the family, and there was little of the difficult times of the past that they wished to discuss. I knew how Daniel viewed it, and it was in fact with considerable wariness that I approached his family at all. But I saw how his parents suffered, how deeply they grieved the loss of their son. Sustaining anger, blame, guilt, and shame aimed at ourselves or others would not bring him back. Painful and emotionally complicated though it will always be to consider the reasons why, the Joneses and I got to know each other.

There is a strong physical resemblance between Daniel and his father, gestures and expressions in common that were difficult for me to watch playing over Mr. Jones's face when I first met him. Daniel's mother was shattered by her son's death, and she and I tried in our different ways to support each other in the months just after his death. We were obsessed with its details, as though repeating it over and over in our minds, backtracking and probing around and reconstructing it would finally allow us to accept it as real. Those who study bereavement know there is a risk that grief-stricken people will become stuck in this phase of mourning, and counsellors gently steer people along this intense course. Yet fixating on the details of the death in the immediate aftermath of it is normal, even necessary for some. It constitutes a means of orienting the wounded heart and mind to the new reality that should not be suppressed.

Over lunches together, Mrs. Jones and I perused photos taken in the months and weeks before the suicide, and pored urgently over the events of Daniel's last days, as if our own lives depended on getting a clear and precise picture. In some ways, they did. We shed tears together. As time went on, we sent letters back and forth, just to keep in touch, sometimes speaking of Daniel and the pain we felt, sometimes just sharing news of our lives. There were visits to the Joneses' home in a small community in southwestern Ontario. On one occasion Mrs. Jones and I knelt on the floor surrounded by photo albums and shoeboxes full of more photos and the usual parents' mementoes of a young son's or daughter's life: This was Daniel when, and here he is again, and again and again. A sweet-looking blond boy, swinging on swings, playing cowboy with his sister, opening Christmas presents, visiting the zoo, off to the high-school formal with a pretty girl.

Mr. Jones was less expressive of his emotions during our visits, yet he struggled to understand too. Ironically, he gave me one of the most tender remembrances of Daniel, as we stood by the open trunk of his car unloading an array of plants from a local nursery. "The first book he ever read was *Mrs. Duck's Lovely Day,*" he told me. Daniel would sit on his lap as a child barely old enough to talk and recite the jolly little tale. He was so bright, Mr. Jones marvelled, so quick to memorize and read, so naturally good at every subject in school.

I ached with sadness listening to this. Such a grim, absurdly long way from *Mrs. Duck's Lovely Day* to *Final Exit,* the suicide recipe book the coroner found resting in plain view on a bookshelf near Daniel's body, the book that so helpfully provided the method of self-destruction Daniel had employed, as well as the template for his suicide note cum last will and testament. I share Dr. Sherwin Nuland's mixed feelings, outlined in his excellent work, *How We Die,* on the place of a book like *Final Exit* in our culture. Its claims of humanitarian concern for the pain of the terminally ill won it a longstanding spot on bestseller lists starting in 1991, and it is still available in glossy paperback. I have found myself hiding it behind other books when I come across it on bookstore shelves, a small personal protest that helps me more than it hurts sales of the book, I am sure. It continues to be implicated in the suicides of more and more depressed people, beyond the terminally ill population for whom it is supposedly intended. I sympathize with those who face lengthy suffering from terminal conditions, and I don't believe in censorship. Still, I find the book's existence and widespread availability an affront.

Now I want to know, how does a person travel in thirty-four

years from such blissful innocence to a state of fear and self-loathing so powerful that it seems the only way out is to die? I know it happens all the time. Some people don't even make it to thirty-four. Some don't even get a grace period from too much knowing in their very infancies. Yes, unconscionable though the thought is, children, too, kill themselves.

Later, in my long quest to understand why this happened to Daniel, why it happens to anyone, I experienced a moment of epiphany while reading Alice Miller's *The Drama of the Gifted Child.* The renowned Swiss psychoanalyst explores the early underpinnings of adult neurosis, all the subtle and intricate familial and social pressures that lead a person from earliest infancy to squash his unique qualities and construct a "false self." This narcissistic self seeks to safely negotiate the world on the world's terms, craves to be loved, but fears to its core that this love, so essential for its very survival, will never be given if the true self is revealed in all its resplendent, yet apparently unacceptable, colours.

To a greater or lesser degree, we all fear this, molding ourselves to fit the place we are given to occupy in the world, however accommodating or untenable it may be. If we're lucky, as we grow into adulthood, we find ways to adjust as necessary to live more comfortably in our own skins, and muster the courage to allow our real selves to emerge for others to accept or reject as they wish. As mature people, we manage to sustain a healthy, balanced sense of self, despite external judgments, good, bad, or indifferent. We know and accept who we really are. The not-so-lucky instead totter along a precarious course, swerving dizzily between inappropriate grandiosity ("I'm *great,* it's the world that's an ass and the cause of all my problems!") and vicious self-hatred ("Could there be a lower form of scum than me?"). Some get stuck in one or the other of these dead-end pathways, or make side-trips down the more dangerous roads of addiction, mania, depression, and suicidality.

But even these hazardous states can eventually be transcended, Miller says. She includes an extraordinary quote from one of her patients, a woman who had survived a serious suicide attempt when she was 28 years old, and reflects at age 40 on how she came to view herself and her life differently over twelve years:

> The world has not changed, there is so much evil and meanness all around me, and I see it even more clearly than before. Nevertheless, for the first time I find life really worth living. Perhaps this is because, for the first time, I have the feeling that I am really living my own life. And that is an exciting adventure. On the other hand, I can understand my suicidal ideas better now, especially those I had in my youth—it seemed pointless to carry on—because in a way I had always been living a life that wasn't mine, that I didn't want, and that I was ready to throw away.

Often, this passage has floated up from memory to comfort and sadden me. On the one hand, it is a testament to the possibility of healing, growth, and transformation, irrefutable proof that a suicidal person can overcome and make sense of his or her self-destructive yearnings. It happens all the time. I've done it myself.

How often I have wished that Daniel could have done it too. In choosing suicide, it seems he was in some way attempting to kill off a false self that no longer served him well, that never had, really. If only the fog of depression clouding his mind had lifted enough in those decisive moments for him to see that it is possible to discard a false self metaphorically, spiritually, that killing off the body that houses the self is literally a case of overkill. It is part of the human condition to transform ourselves. Less violently, we shuck off old ways of being, false or otherwise, and ease into new ones throughout the span of our lives. To let go of the past, however, you have to imagine that something is there to succeed it, and in the end, Daniel, regrettably, lacked that sense. For him, it seems, change equaled trauma, growth equaled terror. In such a state, paralysis and suicidal depression don't seem so out of place.

I believe that for a time, Daniel had faith in the future, but when a pattern of disappointment kindled despair, he felt himself pulled back into the past, overwhelmed by its echoes. Touchingly, he still grappled with the yearning to redo his early years. "Sometimes I feel like I'm 110 years old," he plaintively told me once, "and sometimes I feel about eighteen." Daniel expressed this in his short story "A Torn Ligament," from his last collection, *The People One Knows,* published posthumously:

> I was an alcoholic for ten years. I have not had a drink for six years. The story I am writing is not a complicated one. It has been written before. I am a writer in my early thirties. I want to capture on paper those years when I was still young, before I wanted to be a writer. I want to do this because I wish I could live those years again. I want those years back that I wasted as an alcoholic. I want to be twenty again, not in my early thirties.
>
> The difficulty—and this is why I must rewrite the story, to get this right—is that I can write the story about my past, but I can no longer feel what I felt then. I want to say: This is how it was to be young and to think I was in love. But I no longer know how it was. I cannot remember. If I say, This is why I drank, this is what it felt like to be young and to think I was in love—if I say this—I know that the story will be a better story, but also that it will be a lie.
>
> In the story, the woman whom I call Assa is portrayed as if she does not love the narrator—does not love me. But is it not the alcoholic young man—me—who is unable to love Assa? Is it possible that I was not able to love her, that I hurt and rejected Assa? Could the story have turned out differently? I do not know. I do not know.

Painful as it is to read Daniel's precisely executed fiction, I force myself, and it reveals much. It often strikes me that in his writing, he operated with the cool-eyed detachment of a coroner, performing the autopsy on his own life and dutifully reporting the findings, however unpleasant. To write so clearly of such obsessive solipsism—to observe and comment so subtly on one's own failure of imagination—takes some richness of imagination, an impressive level of creative intelligence. Daniel had to have achieved some protective distance from the self he wrote about in order to perceive the young narrator's dilemma with such acuity. But not quite enough distance, it seems in hindsight, to move safely beyond the emotional paralysis that set in with all that looking backward. In the eyes of a man in a state like that, there could be, literally, no future. It's no coincidence that "no future" was one of the original punk movement's most famous anthemic assertions—a recent book that explored the early years of punk is entitled *Please Kill Me.* Daniel, as a fiercely troubled, talented young man determined to drink himself to death, was inexorably drawn to the scene's nihilism, which he documents with raw force in his novel, also published posthumously, *1978.*

I think of Alice Miller's false-self theory as well when I look at the the last photos of Daniel, taken a few weeks before his death by a friend. There is Daniel, all leather jacket and buckles, his ears multi-pierced, his head recently shaved bald, his demeanor alienated young-mannish. But for me, the Daniel in these pictures is a disturbing pastiche, a jumble. His large, expressive eyes belie the toughness I assume he meant to project. The first time I saw the images, they troubled me, even before his death. The tragically hip image he seemed to aim for simply didn't convince, not me anyway. After his death, the photographs struck me even more as gravely out of kilter, images of a man not sure just who he is or who he wants to be, a thirty-four-year-old who's really eighteen going on 110—a bit of a mess.

Now it is an overcast day in late September, eight months after Daniel's death. I am standing with Mr. and Mrs. Jones at the grave site where their son's ashes are buried, a family plot in a sprawling cemetery in Hamilton, Ontario, where a tree has been planted, and where a salmon-pink marble bench, JONES carved simply into it, sits on the well-tended grass. Jones, of course, is the family name, but also the one-word moniker that Daniel used to go by as a young poet, and with which many are still in the habit of referring to him, though he added "Daniel" later, and regretted having used only his last name as an affectation of youth. (The Library of Congress, he discovered to his chagrin, will not change the names of authors, ever, for any reason, and so he is "Jones" and only "Jones" in that system forever and ever, amen, based on the entry for his first book of poems, *The Brave Never Write Poetry.* Live and learn. His later books appeared with his full name despite this.)

Standing silently at the memorial spot, seeing the name stark like that, it is these echoes I hear, of this old Jones—"Jonesy," even, to some of his former cronies—that Daniel despised and seemed so driven to kill off. No, that Jones was not a very attractive character, although he certainly had his admirers, people who revelled in the outrageous rebellion of the bad-boy poet, the drunk punk who dared pull down his pants at a public reading, who made rude scenes challenging those he found pompous or otherwise objectionable, who wrote defiantly obscene poems, such as the one still considered a classic by some, "Things I Have Put into My Asshole." (These things include the CN Tower.) Though it would without doubt pain Daniel to know, this youthful rant against authority and convention, Toronto-style, written more than a decade earlier, got posted by an anonymous fan on telephone poles and buildings around downtown Toronto after his death, and on several anniversaries thereafter.

Oh, Daniel. I know this is not what you planned, I couldn't help thinking as I stood there, *not what you would have wanted to be most remembered for, nor to rest into eternity in a cemetery in the home town you didn't remember fondly (though where else, I wonder—in an urn sitting on the counter of the Bar Italia, where you used to like to meet people and drink coffee?). It was your friend Kevin Connolly who made a remark to me, a little angry at you and protective of my sanity when I was too far gone in my grief, as a tangled group of friends and colleagues waded through the mire of decisions about how your work would be handled after your death:* "Maybe he should have thought of this and stuck around. I think the living have some rights here."

It saddened me that people who hadn't been a part of Daniel's life for years rushed to publicly eulogize the young man they remembered from ten or twelve years earlier. Of course, they were and are entitled to their memories. I had also known, or more accurately known of, Daniel back in those days, when we were both students at the University of Toronto's University College—we even won the same college literary award one year, a fact that made me laugh when many years later I saw listed on Daniel's résumé the esteemed Norma Epstein Award for Creative Writing. As wide-eyed, bright young things from modest homes in provincial towns, where higher education is not a given, and only a few high school students considered odd in some way leave to pursue it (and to escape feeling odd), we shared the experience of navigating an unfamiliar groves-of-academe world that operated on social formulas and codes of which we were painfully innocent. We traded recollections of our days slouching miserably through the same Victorian hallways with our knapsacks of literary anthologies and fat old novels during the late seventies and early eighties. Daniel's fictionalized account of these years appear in his novel *1978*. If I was a typically gloomy female undergraduate, scribbling my Plath-inspired poems, drawing liberally on all manner of death imagery, Daniel experienced feelings of alienation, anxiety, and depression to a far more alarming degree. Passages of *1978* that describe the narrator at his most stone-drunk and debased, barely able to dress himself properly or function in his job as a kitchen helper at the college's dining hall, are chilling.

Why did this young man carry so much anger? It seemed Daniel by then felt extremely alone, at odds with the steel-town, working-class reality he had recently come from, while furiously unable to fit into the culturally complacent world of middle-class student life, such as it was at a rather stuffy Canadian university that still served afternoon tea in china cups at the genteel Women's Union reception room, and retained its share of ageing, duffer faculty members. It is no wonder that a whip-smart, creative, and undeniably fucked-up boy like Daniel would do the emotional equivalent of sticking his finger in a light socket during these years. He wasn't the only one—*1978* is also a document of the brutal world occupied by young punk wannabes, many of them primally screaming their complicated emotions, produced by family dysfunctions, a fragmented society that seemed to reward the compliant and marginalize the less acquiescent, and in which questing, sensitive young people might well conclude they had "no future." If the alcohol-dazed Daniel found any kind of home in those days, any kind of resonance between his inner self and outer reality, it was in the stark, violent, unforgiving culture of punk.

Our paths hardly ever crossed, except one night at a party I attended in the tiny apartment of a friend in 1982. The place was overflowing with hopelessly jejune university students, mostly in their early twenties. It was hardly a salon soirée or Dadaist happening, but all of us were doing our best to pretend that our avant-garde activities were on a par with those of the artistic denizens of Paris in the twenties, or some other bohemian, and of course better, time and place. There were poetry readings, some dance, or at least, movement, performances, much drinking, and smoking dope. I noticed the tall, skinny, blond guy with rather fierce eyes, the skin dark beneath them, sitting in a chair to the side. I recognized him from around the campus. Tonight he was talking loudly, bossing people around, acting like he owned the place. A young man and woman moved to the centre of the living room and began playing cello and violin. They were not very good, and the little crowd looked bored. The blond man began waving his hands at them like some ill-tempered stage director. "Oh, oh, you're awful," he said, fixing them with a heavy-lidded, contemptuous stare. "That's really bad, do you think you could stop? Really."

I remember being amazed anyone could be so bold and so cutting. Abysmal the pair might have been, but it would have been kinder to just grin and bear it. People began snickering and murmuring among themselves. There was no way the two could continue playing; they quietly packed up their instruments and skulked away. *What an asshole,* I thought. For the rest of the night, he buzzed around, exuding an air of being far above everyone else. In hindsight, I imagine that he was masking the fact that he was scared shitless, of everything and everyone.

"Who was that?" I remember asking a friend some time afterwards. He told me he was Jones, the poet, and regaled me with further tales of his legendarily atrocious, alcohol-fuelled misbehaviour. I was indignant at some of the stories, particularly descriptions of at least one violent public fight with his girlfriend at the time. I told my friend that if he ever hosted another gathering that Jones would be attending, he could count me out.

I forgot about this Jones over the next few years. Eventually, I stumbled on his writing again, found some of it good, some of it not to my taste. I also heard somehow through the grapevine that he had given up drinking, had married, was getting his act together. I would see him now and then bouncing along with his distinctive jackrabbit gait around the College Street West neighbourhood and environs where we had both ended up living. When we met up again in 1993 and I told Daniel of my less than fond memories of him, he was mortified. He said later that he assumed I would never want anything to do with him, and admitted that it was all true, just how bad he was back then. But it was hard to make the connection between the younger, disturbed character I'd heard of and observed myself, and this kind, generous, attentive, rather subdued man in his thirties. Our numerous long and candid conversations convinced me that he had indeed grown and changed.

After his death, every time I read or heard a remembrance that disregarded the man Daniel was trying to become, I marvelled at the blindness that allows someone to imagine that nothing of importance happened in another person's life once they, the eulogizer, were no longer a substantial part of it. While these people mourned the past, I was mourning the present, real time, and a future that was never going to be.

"He was a predator," one woman who had apparently dated Daniel briefly more than a decade earlier was quoted as saying in one newspaper column. I shook my head, recalling the man who had stood on my doorstep one day the previous spring, a box of custard tarts from the Portuguese bakery down the street held in one hand, and a bag of fresh, blushing apricots in the other, how he'd smiled and practically said "Aw, shucks, ma'am," as he handed me these offerings, and came through the door and into the kitchen. He scooped up my cat and began stroking her ears. There was nothing insincere or aggressively louche about this Daniel I got to know. Any revelations about his past behaviour came from his own mouth; he was quite capable of beating himself up over it with no posthumous help from others.

Was it only "Jones," the angry young drunk who would be remembered now? I stared at what seemed to me distorted tributes, and thought of one of the pieces of writing he was working on when he died, an essay on male alcoholic writers. He believed they tended to be celebrated and admired for all the wrong reasons. He had felt his own alcoholism as a yoke, a burden, something he had had to break free of before he could write anything he could respect. I struggled to figure out myself how best to honour the memory of the sober, still conflicted, older man I watched struggling so hard to mature and transform himself. This was one of the cruelest ironies of all surrounding Daniel's suicide, that the old, alcoholic self he did not value, the false self he most wanted to kill off, was the self that was immediately, publicly, ghoulishly, resurrected.

DEAD POET SOCIETY, screamed the headline on the cover of the entertainment weekly *eye,* beside a huge photo of Daniel, two years after his death. In the article, former cronies whinged about his work, in their judgment gone downhill since the heady days of their association with him. From the two-hour conversation I had with the reporter, he extracted one sentence fragment, in which I'd divulged that Daniel left a note tacked to the locked door of the room in which he'd killed himself. The story seemed to have been written, complete with yellowed snapshots, long before the young reporter asked for an interview. Jones the outrageous stalked the world again. It was a sad and incomplete portrayal, a projection of spurious, romantic notions of what it means to live "on the edge," with the appalling implication that once Daniel had stopped abusing himself with alcohol, he lost his inspiration—even, preposterously, "sold out."

It wasn't the first such inane projection to surface. "He could have been a Jean Genet," went one wistful musing in a previous tribute, suggesting that if only he'd been more diligent and patient, he could have realized his talent, and that it was simply a hissy fit over not getting enough attention that had sparked his suicide. When I read this, I thought, what utter horseshit. He could have been Daniel Jones, and that was good enough! I grew irritated with the repulsive drive to situate his death as a literary event, which he in some ways had succumbed to himself. I wanted to shout, Don't you see, it wouldn't have mattered a good goddamn if he never wrote another word—his life had value beyond his literary efforts, and it's a crying shame he didn't see that himself.

These were the raging thoughts that plagued me in the confusion after his death, and again during the week, two years later, when every time I passed a café or corner store, Daniel's photo, trapped with the dead poet society headline in unforgiving newsprint, stared up at me from leftover *eyes* strewn in their racks throughout the city for all to see. I recalled the relaxed July morning that photo was taken by Sam Kanga, a young photographer, with Lynn Crosbie and Clint Burnham posing along with Daniel at the pool tables at the Bar Italia for the cover shot of *The People One Knows*, everyone chatting comfortably, hamming around for the camera. "I've never seen him so serene," Lynn told me that day as we sat sipping coffee afterwards. "When he called and sang 'Happy Birthday' to me on my answering machine, I knew he must be in love," she teased. Her friend was usually so much more reserved and serious, his leisure pastimes more along the lines of perusing the Grand and Toy catalogue, dreaming of new office supplies. Before he'd gone away for the weekend with me in Killarney, he had called Lynn to tell her that he was doing this unusual thing, perhaps hoping for moral support and sisterly approval from a fellow depressive. "Your books and catalogues will still be there when you get back," Lynn had counselled. "Just go have some fun."

Now I avert my eyes from that summertime photo of Daniel the serene. "Don't let other people taint the sense of love and significance you feel about your time with Daniel," advises Daniel's psychiatrist. "He loved you," he assures me. But this is not much comfort, no shield against others' twisted, hurtful perceptions.

Contemplating the long remove between the fantasies people have about death, especially suicide, and the paradoxical reality of it always saddens and angers me. Daniel, of all people, understood how little glory there is in depressive illness, and admitted to the end that he feared pain and regretted what he was doing, even as he did it, arguing to himself and anyone who read his note that he had no other option. Yet possibly he wished to the end that he could still, maybe, find one. A poet from Daniel's former circle began cynically referring to his suicide as a "career move." He even wrote a bitter little poem about it. It appalled me that someone who'd once counted himself a friend of Daniel's would display such callous disregard for his final tragedy, but it should not have surprised me. People naturally seek to distance themselves from horror with this kind of glib, black humour. It is easier to bend someone into unflattering caricature without thought for the impact it might have on those he knew and loved.

Several rumours circulated after Daniel's death: He had just found out he had AIDS; he had plagiarized his forthcoming book of short stories; he'd been seriously hitting the bottle for months, and had been spotted getting hammered in various bars; as editor of the literary magazine, *Paragraph*, he'd planned to include in the last issue he edited before his death a series of photographs taken by a friend in which she depicts herself as a character in various suicidal poses. Actually, Daniel had long admired her surreal and haunting photography on a wide range of themes. She has since won international acclaim for her work. She later told me how stunned she was to be approached by someone who remarked, "I guess you must feel bad about those photos," as if they had somehow instigated her friend's suicide. Had someone also relayed to me that Daniel had been spotted slaughtering goats on the waterfront one midnight by the full moon, I would not have been surprised.

It was hard to take the rumours seriously, disheartening to imagine them believed. When the coroner's report from the obligatory autopsy cited "traces" of alcohol, some swooped in to say "Aha!" The finding confirms nothing. There was no alcohol in Daniel's apartment, save mouthwash and possibly cough medicine, and Daniel hadn't left the place for several days before his death. He was no Aqua Velva man (Hermit Sherry had been his plonk of choice at his worst point a decade earlier), though he might have gargled. It would have been difficult for someone who hadn't had a drink in eight years to suddenly start a wild binge, yet hide it entirely from someone with whom he had almost daily contact. There is no good cause for such speculation; at most, Daniel's fear, justified or not, that he might return to a life of alcoholism would have been just another reason in his mind to kill himself.

For some, though, suicide equals melodrama. There must be some obvious cause and effect, some single coherent reason why it happened, someone to accuse. I was myself accused of all manner of baroque nastiness, from murder to bad manners, and of anonymously penning a story sympathetic to Daniel and critical of his publisher in the national satirical magazine, *Frank*. To this day, I have no idea who wrote the curious squib in question. It might have been well meant, but was filled with sloppy factual errors, and caused more problems than it solved.

When the prosaic truth fails to live up to expectations, overheated imaginations are brought into play. This impulse to embellish is linked, I think, to the ambivalence we all feel, yet may not wish to acknowledge, about the person who has left this way, surely making a statement, a damning comment, a "take *that*," or a "woe is me, and here is the final proof." It's easier to respond with a black-and-white theory, to fashion a coherent narrative momentum and linear chronology for the person's life, which stops with the resounding THE END of his suicide—and the epilogue containing the final judgments of the living.

"Ah, the 'pitchfork'/'halo' scenario," said Karen Letofsky, executive director of the Survivor Support Programme in Toronto, during a counselling session after Daniel's death. There was comfort in learning that these kinds of stark, cartoonish reactions are quite common, as people seek to either sanctify the deceased or throw him into the burning fires of hell. Short shrift is given to the irresolute, contradictory nature of suicide—the person's motives, the circumstances surrounding the event, our responses.

If the living must live with mere interpretations, speculative and incomplete, they must also live with a burning curiosity about just how the person who did the deed interpreted the suicide himself. This is certainly the case in the period immediately following the death. Marc Etkind, author of a slim yet astonishing volume of collected suicide notes entitled . . . *Or Not To Be,* describes himself as a television documentary producer who, "except for a handful of coroners and psychologists . . . has probably read more suicide notes than anyone else," and suggests that virtually everyone on the verge of suicide, certainly those who leave notes behind, has a distorted perception of what he or she is doing, and the impact the suicide will have.

> If suicide notes are indeed attempts at communication, then they are dismal failures. We all hope that as we near death, we'll have a moment of understanding, where our thoughts crystallize and we can sum up our existence with eloquence. But if the suicide attempter had this moment of understanding, he probably wouldn't kill himself. And there lies the ultimate paradox of the suicide note: If someone could think clearly enough to leave a cogent note, that person would probably recognize that suicide was a bad idea. Or as Edwin Shneidman writes, "In order to commit suicide, one cannot write a meaningful note; conversely, if one could write a meaningful note, one would not have to commit suicide." Suicide notes, written when people are at their psychological worst, are anything but the voice of clarity. Instead they are bizarre, rambling, angry and, above all, sad documents of disturbed minds.

While I agree that people who kill themselves are at their psychological worst, I would also argue that the notes they leave behind are not entirely meaningless. A suicide note can be rife with meaning—just not the one solely intended by the deceased. It would be hard to top "Dear Betty, I hate you. Love, George," one of the shortest notes Etkind includes in the book, for succinct conveyance of a point; indeed, the essential marrow of meaning at the heart of an entire life, that may have eluded both poor George and Betty, but not a distant reader of such a compact novel in a note.

However dubious on an emotional level, suicide notes require a certain degree of rationality to write, and have been recognized in law numerous times as "holographic" wills, that is, legitimate statements of the last wishes of the deceased. It is this principle that guides the concise instructions for writing a suicide note in the form of a legitimate will in *Final Exit*. And so, Daniel, capable of reading a book, absorbing the information it contained, and acting on it, was executing a relatively straightforward series of physical steps in a logical fashion, including the writing of a suicide note. In it he says that he hadn't planned to write it, just scribbled it "off the cuff." It does not surprise me that Daniel, being a writer, would join the fewer than one in five suicides, according to Etkind, who leave suicide notes. And for someone who had not intended to write a note, he certainly picked up a head of steam quickly enough upon beginning the task. Along with its expressions of self-loathing and extreme psychological suffering, the note is filled with instructions that detail, with characteristic punctiliousness, if not always straightforward logic, what he wanted done with his work. He also revealed his self-doubts: "To plan my final publications is a bit self-centred—I will be dead; the work may not be any good."

Difficult though reading this in the days after his death was, it was Daniel's situating of his suicide in a literary context that I found hardest to accept. I empathize with any writer's frustration, even despair, over how difficult it is to fashion a writer's life, particularly in Canada, where to sell a few thousand copies of a work of fiction or poetry is to be a roaring success, and to sell a few hundred is more the norm. Yet I cannot accept that this was worth dying for. Nor can I accept Daniel's placement of his suicide in linked formation with suicides of the past (he dedicated his note to the late Robert Billings, another Canadian poet who combated mental problems and killed himself amid a turmoil of bad relations with friends and publishing colleagues), thereby somehow dignifying the act beyond its depressive underpinnings. In this, I believe Daniel was dead wrong. Others too viewed Daniel's suicide as in some way redeemed by its larger literary import, even went so far as to hope that his suicide note would eventually be published as a literary text, a final addition to his oeuvre.

I found it all offensive. The one thing I will not do is make Daniel's death lyrical. There is nothing exalted about death, particularly suicide. It is grossly physical, ugly, and monstrously intrusive, from the finding, removal, and identification of the body, to the autopsy, the funerals,and memorial services, the morbid tasks that must be performed far longer than anyone imagines could possibly be endured. Suicide is also so terribly banal, the moment of death itself mechanical, mundane, more anticlimactic than anyone's "Goodbye, Cruel World" fantasies would have it. I think most of us, in our death-denying culture, don't like to ponder how close our living selves are always, potentially, to death. How fragile we are. One moment, a man is standing in his bathroom flossing his teeth, or filling a coffee pot at the kitchen counter; the next, he is downing an overdose of pills and placing a plastic bag over his head; moments later, life unceremoniously transforms to death. Daniel's autopsy report itself I only scanned quickly before stuffing it into a file folder for good, and have had to block it from my mind. The thought of a young body clinically invaded that way, let alone one I knew intimately, surpasses my ability or desire to imagine.

It is the living who must cope with the horror and absurdity of it all. One of the most helpful books I read in the aftermath of Daniel's death was *Words I Never Thought to Speak,* a collection of interviews with suicide survivors at various stages of their grieving. For me, the most moving and comforting anecdotes were those that revealed the awkward and ludicrous moments that seem so at odds with the magnitude of the tragedy: Imagine Alvin and the Chipmunks singing Wagner's Ring Cycle. My heart went out to the son who told of how his family sat in charged silence as they drove to Dad's funeral, in the car in which he had only days earlier gassed himself to death; the young bride who, after scattering the ashes of the man she'd married less than a year earlier, stands by the ocean, wondering anxiously what to do with the plastic baggie that had contained them. Who wouldn't feel for the daughter of poet Anne Sexton, agonizing over whether to honour her mother's quixotic wish to have the palindrome "Rats live on no evil star" as her gravestone's epitaph? (After much soul searching, the young woman, who'd endured her flamboyantly narcissistic mother's suicidal behaviour from childhood until her late teens, when Sexton finally succeeded in killing herself, in the end opted against it. It is hard to fault her in that decision.)

Now, I can only conclude that if Daniel the writer put his faith entirely in words, placing his very life in their power, Daniel the man was summarily betrayed by them. I believe he might still be alive if he had learned to define himself as something more than a writer—as "something human," to quote the final words of his short story "A Torn Ligament." To me, there is one thing he did reveal in his final note, in the very fact that he wrote it at all. As he sat in that dark corner of his life, feeling lost without words, taking pen to paper, he asked that his grammar and spelling be cleaned up (he was acknowledging the growing influence of the tranquillizers he had swallowed before he sat down to write), should anyone ever publish the note. He envisioned a future, even if he did not imagine that he would be there. It mattered to him enough to try to shape that future in some small way, with words, to the end.

Those who write of the future must possess a shred of hope and faith, a sense of connection, that there are things they would like to have happen, and things they would not. And anyone with this hope, no matter how strong their desire to die, probably also harbours somewhere within themselves a desire to live. Whether he intended it to or not, Daniel's suicide note, all twenty-one scribbled squares of notepaper, tells me that. Yet whatever future Daniel imagined, it was not the one that came to pass. Ultimately, words failed him.

Eventually, I accepted that just as the dead typically don't get all their wishes, or leave the legacy they envisioned, if they envisioned one at all, so their survivors cannot control what people say or think of the event either. This is nowhere more obvious than in the extraordinary case of the late English poet Ted Hughes, who wrote publicly in his 1997 collection *Birthday Letters,* for the first time in thirty-seven years, and in the year of his own death from cancer, about his wife Sylvia Plath's life and suicide. In an article accompanying excerpts from the book in *The New Yorker,* his friend and colleague Alfred Alvarez wrote that Hughes was always grimly aware of being, in his own words, "a projection post" for the many who preferred their own invented narratives, with him as unmitigated villain, to the thorny truth. Hughes was right: The sweeping condemnation of him, driven by what seems a childish, knee jerk-feminist spin on the tragedy, went into full throttle on several chat sites and forums on the Internet after the publication of *Birthday Letters,* as the incensed gathered to discuss the scourge of Hughes, and further sanctify the divine Sylvia.

These people have forgotten that the woman they so admire attempted suicide long before she met Hughes, and wrote compellingly about her youthful depression in her powerful novel *The Bell Jar.* As Germaine Greer suggests in her study of female poets, *Slip-Shod Sybils,* Plath wrote in the context of a female aesthetic of self-destruction, well developed by then, that nurtured her primal urge toward death. Plath was profoundly, pathologically depressed, living in a cold, foreign country, feeling alone and overwhelmed by motherhood and marital difficulties. She had easy access to a means to an end. The famous poet was not the only person to die by household oven, before the lethal gas that made it possible was removed from the mix by the companies that produced it.

For some reason, we often forget that writers are in fact also human beings. I sometimes wonder whether the notion that writers suffer from depression in greater proportion than others is wrong-headed. Is it not only that because they are writers, they write about their experience, finding expression for their pain in a way that a nurse, a policeman, a dentist, or an abused aboriginal foster child would not? The gifted Sylvia Plath expressed her darkness and pain with accomplished literary brilliance. Yet, regardless of her ability to articulate her experience in language that would be widely admired, even revered as a result of her tragedy, she was still a young woman suffering from what we call depression. In this she was quite ordinary.

Given what I know of surviving suicide, no one need worry that Ted Hughes didn't suffer enough. (His second wife also killed herself, murdering their three-year-old child before doing so.) His pain and his love for his former wife radiate through *Birthday Letters*. It is a work of grand and astonishing intimacy I found deeply moving. During my most intense grief over Daniel, it did occur to me painfully that while I would one day be an old woman, Daniel would remain forever the young man he was when he died. In my ageing memory, he will inevitably change, and I wondered how he will seem to me as time passes. Even after five years, I think of him in a more distanced way, as a younger man I once knew, whose plight I witnessed and which still elicits sorrow and pity. Though his death is no longer the centre of my life, he holds a place in my heart, despite changes in my life, my relationships, my shifting self.

Often, after an apparently sudden suicide, people say things like, "We had no idea he was *that far gone.*" The difficult truth is, maybe he, or she, wasn't. Maybe that person has lived through far worse times, but this time, there was a gun handy. Maybe just a momentary feeling, a perverse and bleak impulse coupled with a convenient means removes a person from life when a moment later, the same person might have reconsidered, as he or she has countless times before. Living with depression and suicidal feelings is like that. The man who lost his desire to jump from the Golden

Gate Bridge the moment he'd done it was lucky to live. Countless people reconsider mid-attempt, begin to approach an awareness that the act, however firm or feeble, is metaphorical in some way, the proverbial cry for help, and live to be thankful they did.

The recent, award-winning Iranian film *A Taste of Cherry,* an unusually subtle cinematic exploration of suicide, makes this point powerfully. The main character, a middle-aged man who no longer sees the point of living, drives through the desolate Iranian landscape surrounding Teheran in a Range Rover, picking up three different passengers he hopes will bury his body by the side of the road once he has killed himself. All three refuse his strange request, and in the course of their rides with the suicidal protagonist, they engage him in philosophical debate over the question of whether to be or not to be, arguing persuasively for the former.

His final passenger, a grizzled, gravel-voiced old man, relates the story of his own attempted suicide, when he was a younger man, eking out a marginal existence with his family on a failing farm. He had gotten up one day at dawn, walked with a rope to a nearby orchard, and climbed into a cherry tree. He fashioned his noose, placed it around his neck preparing to jump from the limb, when he noticed the exquisite ripe fruit suspended from a nearby branch glowing in the morning light. He was captured by the beauty of the succulent blossoming clusters and could not resist popping one in his mouth. As he felt the cherry burst against his teeth, he was filled with sensual bliss, and knew in that instant that he did not want to die. Instead, he dismantled his noose, picked a handful of berries, and carried them home, where he placed them in a bowl and took them to the bed where his wife still lay sleeping. The woman was lulled into the day by the delightful scent of the fruit he had brought her, never knowing what a momentous turn of events her husband's gentle act represented. "A cherry saved my life," says the wise old man, with a can-you-believe-it? shrug, to the suicidal one.

Abbas Kiarostami's extraordinary film is banned in Iran; strict Islamic law, like most religions, forbids suicide, and the censors there fail to see that a film like this might be one of the most powerful suicide prevention messages they could allow to be disseminated. Secular and modern in tone and presentation, its wisdom apparently cannot be allowed voice among people who would surely find themselves reflected there.

In contemporary Western culture, Spalding Gray's tragicomic musings on suicide are as wise and revealing as any. Gray has spent his life in the shadow of his mother's suicide, a grim reality he explores to great humorous effect in his monologue *Monster In A Box.* In his later work, *It's A Slippery Slope,* he recounts a moment out hiking on a high cliff with his girlfriend, when he feels a nearly irresistible urge to leap over the edge. He was not particularly depressed at the time, he just feels the seductive pull of the abyss more strongly than most others, the option of suicide never far from the edge of his consciousness, perhaps utterly central to it, something he is compelled to dance incessantly around. What stops him in the end is the look of horror he imagines would cross his girlfriend's face as he hung momentarily in the air just before falling to his death. With comic self-mockery, he implies that it may be more his feeling that he couldn't live with that on his conscience for the last few seconds of his life, than concern for his girlfriend, that stops him. He saunters peacefully on, his girlfriend oblivious to all that just didn't happen.

These particular contemplations of suicide struck a deep chord in me. They reveal the uncomfortable truth that all around us, within us, at any time, more lives than we care to imagine hang in the balance, spiritually, emotionally. Who can say what small blessing or absurdity will determine the ultimate call? Many who live with suicidal feelings say that, ironically, it is only the comforting knowledge that if their pain became too great to bear they could end their lives that gives them the strength to carry on living. Without that imagined escape hatch, they say they would succumb to paralyzing despair, rather than the mild to chronic depression that defines most of their days.

Yet the immutable fact of a suicide seems to herald our worst assumptions about the person's mental state, the horrible things that must have driven him or her to it. But this doesn't answer the question of why it is that many people live through the most abysmal realities, surviving with grace and courage, while others seem unable to cope with comparatively mild adversity. Some people will live with depression and its disastrous fallout for years, never acting on suicidal feelings, doing so perversely at a time when life seem to be going better than ever for them.

It is a less than encompassing general understanding of the some-times depressingly flimsy and random dynamics of suicide that has made many a suicide survivor, particularly parents, feel tarred and feathered by social stigma that carries an implicit accusation: Your son/daughter killed him or herself, therefore whatever happened in your family must have been infinitely worse than what happens in families where all the kids survive. It isn't quite so simple. Certainly, it's difficult to dispute the link between childhood adversity and adult emotional troubles that can lead to suicide. "That the early social environment of suicidal individuals is often markedly disorganized is well established in an extensive literature on suicide and attempted suicide," writes psychiatrist Kenneth S. Adam of the University of Toronto in a 1986 article entitled "Early Family Influences on Suicidal Behavior," in the journal *Annals New York Academy of Sciences*. "Disorganized" in this context may mean, explains Adam, "marital conflict, parental hospitalization, parental alcoholism, and mental illness . . . along with the more obvious family disruptions caused by parental deaths, separations, and divorce. More subtle variables such as covert hostility, isolation, and rejection by parents have also been found."

Distinguished pioneer suicidologist Ed Shneidman, in his 1996 book, *The Suicidal Mind*, brilliantly condenses a four-decade career's worth of observations and reflections, based on literally thousands of "psychological autopsies" and case studies of suicide. He writes, powerfully:

I am totally willing to believe that suicide can occur in adults who could not stand the immediate pain of grief or loss that faced them, independent of a good or bad childhood or good or bad parental care and love. But I am somewhat more inclined to hold to the view that the subsoil, the root causes of being unable to withstand those adult assaults lie in the deepest recesses of personality that are laid down in rather early childhood. . . . It is not possible to be robbed totally of one's childhood, but what does happen can seem to be just as bad. One can have one's childhood vandalized. Perhaps—I do not know—every person who commits suicide, at *any* age, has been a victim of a vandalized childhood, in which that preadolescent child has been psychologically mugged or sacked, and has had psychological needs, important to that child, trampled on or frustrated by malicious, preoccupied, or obtuse adults.

Obviously, it would be painful for a parent to read such words after the suicide of a child. In many cases, hard observations like these of Adam and Shneidman are without a doubt true. But in what family is there not some amount of covert hostility? If divorce in and of itself caused suicide, the suicide rate would be catastrophically higher. Clearly, there are subtleties here that have to be taken into account when drawing conclusions about cause and effect involving suicide. I have met many loving parents devastated by the suicides of their young sons and daughters, parents who were not alcoholics, not divorced, not malicious vandalizers of their children's early years—including parents of offspring with such illnesses as schizophrenia or manic depression, who did everything humanly possible to help their suffering children before losing them in cruel and violent ways; and parents who, in the wake of their personal tragedies, were motivated to educate themselves and help others.

It has been in part that frustrating sense felt by many survivors of suicide that they have been condemned, misunderstood, and neglected by mental-health professionals that has led them to form their own support groups over the past decade or so. Now, their numbers and degree of organization amount to a vocal movement. Not surprisingly, while more doctors, social workers, and bereavement specialists are gaining a greater understanding of the unique aspects of grief experienced by survivors of suicide, tensions exist between the two groups, and they were obvious at the conference of the American Association of Suicidology conference I attended in Memphis in 1997. At times, I felt like a double agent. As a journalist, I found that doctors and counsellors of all kinds were willing to speak to me, and even though I was upfront about also being a suicide survivor, they were frank in airing reservations about allowing what has been an organization of professionals in many disciplines, researching all aspects of suicide, to include a new contingent of mostly lay people whose chief focus is their own loss and bereavement. Meanwhile, survivors warmly welcomed me into their comforting circles, and spoke openly of their own concerns about the condescending desire for exclusivity of some of the professionals.

I came to feel that both groups had their points. Sometimes, watching the psychologists, psychiatrists, and social workers make their complicated presentations, complete with dizzying successions of graphs and bar charts projected onto screens, I wondered if they hadn't strayed a little too far from the humanity of the people that were the ostensible focus of all this theorizing. On the other hand, I was taken aback to learn that a group of survivors wished to reroute the AAS quarterly research journals that came to them automatically when they joined the organization, from their homes directly to local libraries, because they found reading them "upsetting." Better they go to libraries than into the garbage, but I did wonder if this wasn't a variation on a Groucho Marx joke about masochism—why join a club whose members espouse ideas you have no interest in exploring, or outright reject before you've even considered them? Perhaps both sides need to sit down and listen to each other with more open minds, and concede a few points; sometimes a suicidal person's best hope is medical intervention, but sometimes too, all the drugs and professional expertise in the world can't stop a suicide. Sometimes parents do indeed break their children's spirits; and sometimes, children of decent, loving parents kill themselves too. Not one of us has the definitive answer to all the questions that still surround suicide.

Each person grows in the world with a unique combination of genetic propensities, environmental influences, familial relationships borne along on wonderful and dreadful moments, and a relationship to society that may be nurturing or destructive, depending on how the former factors play themselves out. Of course, it benefits everyone to minimize the things in life that cause emotional pain—the unholy trinity of child abuse, addiction, poverty, numerous other related ills—to educate ourselves about the signs that a person may be depressed or suicidal, and to know how to act if so. It's a matter of paying attention, of taking the time to develop an understanding of how complex suicide can be. Social and cultural conditions beyond family can indeed play a part in tipping someone over the emotional edge and into the suicide danger zone: Fisheries fail, leaving entire towns with skyrocketing suicide rates. Gambling fuels economic development, street drugs and guns proliferate, and we see the casualties rise. Japan's suicide rate has escalated in the wake of its recently plummetting economy.

Focussing only on organic, individual causes for suicide to the exclusion of all other factors, and scurrying away in fear and dismissal from social responsibilities and community interventions, will not make it go away. Many people want to uphold a blinkered biological approach to depression: We live in an age of antidepressants of ever-more-refined design, yet the suicide rate is not commensurately lower. If all it took was a pill, a lot of people now dead would be walking around alive and well, perhaps including Daniel, who was on antidepressants at the time of his death. Drugs do play a role for many people, but they are not necessarily the entire answer to a person's malaise. A suicidal person may pitch from doctor to doctor, pill to pill, only to find his or her appetite for life restored by a lucky break on a job, a new relationship, an unexpected turn of fortune for the better. Touching stories abound, like that of the heroin addict in Winnipeg, who while walking down a street in rock-bottom despair one day, heard the cries of an old woman in a burning house, and without thinking ran through the thick smoke to break a basement window and pull the woman out. Interviewed later, her face glowed with pride and astonishment that she, the worst person on earth in her own eyes, had saved a life—two, including her own. Six weeks after the event, she was clean of drugs, and still visiting the grateful old woman. A depressed mother of two toddlers wrote a letter to Oprah Winfrey, telling her that she was just in the process of putting her kids to bed so that she could kill herself, when she happened to hear the talk-show host interviewing Maya Angelou. Something the poet said struck such a chord, the woman fell to the floor sobbing in gratitude, no longer wishing to die. Corny, but better than years of Prozac.

I write this at a time when the government of the province in which I live, Ontario, is closing several mental-health treatment clinics for children and dismantling a host of related services designed especially for emotionally disturbed children and adolescents. Even the provincial government's own child advocate has said publicly that the state of mental-health-care services for children is "in crisis," and that the lack of proper childhood care often leads to later tax-burdensome incarceration in correctional institutions. The untreated mentally ill or emotionally disturbed eventually lash out. We are regressing in dealing with these matters, in a way that can only lead to more tragedy.

Still, with every good intention, and adequately funded, well-designed and managed public mental health programs in place, we cannot definitively predict who will be felled by suicidal feelings and who will overcome them. As with something as basic and lifesaving as cardiopulminary resuscitation (CPR), we can train people to know what to do in a suicidal crisis. At the same time, suicide prevention training for individuals will not in and of itself reduce the prevalence of those factors that lead to suicide, any more than prepping a population to know how to massage suddenly failing hearts can do much to stop people from doing things that lead to heart attacks. As with CPR, when it comes to suicide there is no guarantee that someone with the knowledge to prevent it will be around when the crisis happens. I have met people from families plagued by suicide, in which every member was an alcoholic or drug addict except that one person; people who have survived unspeakable torture in prisons foreign and domestic, severe sexual abuse, violent assaults, their own addictions, and yet who maintain a happy view of life, or have recovered enough to reach out to others. I have met people who have shown me photo after photo of their beloved dead, a person unmolested or traumatized in any obvious way, who put a gun to his head after a romantic rejection or a failed exam or a rough call from a collection agency about a credit-card debt.

I recall suicidal moments of my own, several months after Daniel's death. I had gone to dinner at a friend's. It had been a lovely evening of good company and good food. The moment I was alone again, heading home, a frightening numbness set in, and a blunt thought crossed my mind: *If I had a gun, I would shoot myself right now. Why not? What is the point of anything?* The aggressive impulse was strong and lasted well after I got home and had crawled into bed. What saved me, aside from not having a gun, was the fact that part of me knew why I was having these feelings. By then, I had read of how common it was for people to feel suicidal after a loved one's suicide. I recognized it as a passing part of the grief.

If I'm honest, I realize it was a feeling I have had before in my life, long ago, in my twenties, that same disconcerting "I'm fine as long as I'm with people, desperate when alone" chronic depression, complete with "suicidal ideation" that had beset me for several terrifying months. So when it reappeared, even briefly, I knew I had to, and could, wait it out. Who knows where this strength comes from, what allows people to go on? But it did. I did. It's not something to feel smugly proud of, it is simply a reality. Those feelings vividly recalled, although experienced so long ago during that youthful depression, that primal darkness that seemed to seep through my blood, slowing me, making me turn hatred on myself, had a weird and horrible power. Then, as mysteriously and randomly as they had arrived, the feelings dissipated to nothingness. Eventually I could say I was no longer depressed, and could tell the difference between depression and grief, ordinary sadness and a hormone-driven PMS fit of teariness, anxiety, and irritability. This is what living with depression means. Not necessarily getting rid of it, or its potential to return, but learning to know it, identify it, grapple with it like an old enemy, let it run its course, refuse to give it the upper hand. Millions of people learn to do this. Daniel did, too, for a while.

I can probably anticipate that Daniel will always be with me, somehow, and that at times, I will find myself addressing him directly. Nearly everyone I have spoken with who has lost someone to suicide admits that at some time or other, perhaps quite regularly, they speak to their dead. More than three decades after his wife's death at age 30, Ted Hughes, then in his late 60s, still addressed her directly—the poems are almost all to "you," the beloved, troubled, and tragically lost Sylvia. He imagined a dialogue with her, an eternal bond. In these fiercely loving poems, there is the world, and then there they are, separate from it, together on their own small planet, Ted and Sylvia, sharing a unique, intimate knowledge. And so it is expressed, in a poet's tough and beautiful language, this searing truth—as the living person's narrative moves along, the absent person remains vibrantly real, a thread, thinning perhaps as time unfolds, new relationships evolve, and old age encroaches, but strong as spun gold nonetheless, running through the story that continues to write itself.

For better or for worse, denied or acknowledged, that connection to the dead is an integral part of the survivor's life.

January 1994. We go to see a movie called *True Romance*. We eat dinner first, sharing a dish of Love Spice Shrimp in a Vietnamese restaurant near the theatre on Bloor Street west of Ossington. It's freezing outside. We shiver and run. We sit in the balcony, you put your arm around me. My hand languishes comfortably over your knee. We like the movie. We talk about it in the cafe next door afterwards. You wonder whether it has achieved Baudrillard's fifth simulation. I can't help laughing and teasing you about the pretentiousness of such a statement, and soon, you are laughing too. Words flow easily, endlessly between us. We run back to your apartment, cursing the cold. "I feel so close to you," you say with intensity, as we lie huddled together.

What is it that we gave each other, anyway? What is it that we "loved"? How did we manage it when we encountered each other, when our broken attempts at lasting connection pitched us back into the unenviable state of searching singlehood, our longings and regrets rather too obvious to ourselves and, we suspected, to others, despite our brave faces? Somehow we did manage it. Even though in the beginning we might have doubted that we had anything of value to offer, there were found bits and pieces, discarded or neglected parts of ourselves we might have forgotten or never realized were there at all. Suddenly, we saw these things in each other with exquisite clarity, and weren't afraid to feel again as we picked them up like unexpected treasures on a beach, and let them shimmer and play in the new light. It is difficult to understand why or how this happened. When it did, we couldn't believe our luck. It was the thrilling, elusive thing we all hope for, that deep erotic bonding between lovers, and compared by every modern psychologist from Freud on, to the "oceanic" feelings between mothers and infants. Babies must bond to survive; in "romantic" love, adults seek to duplicate the wonderfully fulfilling sensations of that long-ago connection. On rare occasions, it goes beyond the sexual and hits on something far more profound. It's what is missing from those dreary, awkward dates from which we slink away with mutual embarrassment, to crawl into our beds alone, telling ourselves wryly that it might be best to pack in this fruitless search, imagining that the kind of connection that we want, that we dream of, does not exist.

For a time with you, Daniel, it did. That you should choose to die in the midst of such hope and promise, such renewed faith in life and its possibilities, is for me the saddest thing of all.

You killed yourself a month after that lovely, light evening. This is not something a person "gets over." It is just something I live with.

May 1994. I am driving west along Bloor Street. It's warm and sunny. Chestnut trees are blooming and swaying in the light breeze, and though I am still caught in grief I notice that it makes me happy, somehow, the sun, the balmy wind, the blossoming trees and flowers after such a long and terrible winter. I know it would do nothing for you, or so you always claimed about your indifference to trees and other simple, natural beauties.

Without warning, I catch sight of the theatre in the distance as I approach Dovercourt Road. Suddenly I feel a confused dread, remembering what might have been the last good time out we had together, when we talked and talked, and you said you felt so close to me. So close. What *did* you mean? If you were still alive, I'd know. Or at least I would have the innocent luxury of imagining I did.

I see for the first time that the theatre is called The Paradise. Some strange sound comes from my mouth when I also see on the marquee, where a movie title should be, three words stacked on top of each other:

WE

NEVER

DIE

I forget about the chestnut trees, the warm, gentle air. As I pass the theatre, I am leaning slightly in my seat against the door, resting my elbow out the window, my hand holding my head, my fleeting springtime serenity dissolved. I'm resisting something, as if I can't decide whether what just happened is terrible or comforting.

It's both.

Thanks for the ironies, sweetheart.

Your parents and I don't say much as we stand awkwardly together at the place where your ashes are buried. What is there to say? Eventually, we get back in the car and begin driving along the gently looping roads of the vast, pristine graveyard, all whispers, cut grass and carved stone. Your mother is crying. I sit in the back seat trying to hold back my own tears. Your father looks over at your mother, with an expression on his face so like yours. He reaches over to put his arm around her.

I close my eyes.

DOING TIME
IN THE PRISON OF MOURNING

JUNE 1993. IN A COLLEGE STREET fruit and vegetable market, I watch Daniel as he carefully selects tomatoes and places them in a bag, absorbed in his task, his expression peaceful, lit by something. Could it possibly be happiness, that "rare, infectious bliss" Lynn described in her poem?

"I have never been able to live, except the occasional brief moment, without a sense of horror, disgust, self-loathing," Daniel wrote in his suicide note. Was this one of those moments? As I study his face, his astonishing eyes, their impossible shade of aqua blue, his sleek, flaxen hair pulled back in a ponytail, my affection turns in a flickering second to an awareness, in some way terrible, of how quickly Daniel has opened himself to me, more quickly and completely than I have to him. It's he who cries over his past, I who comfort; once, when Daniel leaned against me in his sorrow, I felt overwhelmed by his call for emotional first aid, not sure which wound to treat first. There were so many.

Standing there regarding Daniel, I am struck by a wave of intense emotion; more than anything—remarkably, as I see it now—a harrowing sense of the man's vulnerability ambushes me, the same feeling of awe I feel when holding a newborn, or staring into a box of puppies, a primal sense of duty to protect, also the power to harm.

My next thought, a vivid flash, is: *You must never hurt him.* As though I had extra responsibilities here, of an adult to a child, or at least, of a stronger being to a weaker one. Yet I know it isn't possible to be close to someone and not hurt that person, sooner or later, even if you don't consciously want to. "Sometimes we hurt each other just by being alive and different," my wise friend Laima once said. Could a person be as fragile as Daniel seems in this strange, charged moment, and survive the ordinary ups and downs of any life, any relationship? Why does this grown man kindle such a fierce, maternal urge in me?

I hurry away from the moment, burying its uncomfortable revelations as quickly as I can, returning my attention to the mushrooms and lettuce and green peppers heaped around us. When Daniel and I emerge onto the street with our bags of groceries, we are both smiling.

February 1994. I am sitting at a table in the Palmerston Library, perusing a pharmaceutical compendium, researching an article I'm writing about the antidepressant Prozac. Out of interest, I flip to the page that describes the antidepressant that Daniel takes, an older form of drug called an MAO inhibitor. He had tried Prozac, but it had failed to treat his symptoms as effectively. Here are listed potential side effects, always unsettling reading, regardless of the medication. I feel a surge of alarm as I scan through one of this particular drug's provisoes: People taking it should not eat cheese, which contains a chemical that can react badly, even fatally, with a chemical in the drug. Didn't we have lasagna for dinner last night? I recalled that Daniel had mentioned this prohibition before, yet he ate the cheese-laden meal.

Comically, as I see it now, I rush from the library to a pay phone and quickly punch Daniel's number, burbling to him about this cheese business, and is he feeling all right? Daniel laughs and says, "No, no, it's *aged* cheeses that are the problem. Mozzarella and ricotta are okay." I feel relieved, and a little foolish. "Don't worry about me," he reassures me. "I've lived with this for a long time. I know how to take care of myself."

We have this conversation roughly one week before his suicide. It is also during the weeks of late January and early February that he is getting seriously discouraged about his writing career. He is anxious about the disastrous state of his financial affairs: his student loans and interest, accumulated over many years, looming larger than ever, his credit cards maxed out, his income meagre and not looking up since he was laid off a part-time job as a creative writing instructor at York University earlier in the year. Apart from the forthcoming publication of his book of short stories, it seems there is little light at the end of the tunnel—and all this piled onto his deeply rooted and complicated feelings about success and failure. This was something he wrote about with bleak humour in his fiction; it is possible for intelligent people to be keenly aware of their emotional problems, yet unable to solve them. The current psychotherapy industry, not to mention Woody Allen's career as a filmmaker, runs on that truth.

It was during this time, too, on a day when Daniel received another rejection letter from an arts-grant committee, that he collapsed on the bed beside me, sighed deeply, and said, "You know, you should leave me. I mean for your sake, you should get the hell out, because I'm going straight down the tubes, I'm telling you that." He continued in this self-disparaging vein, saying how it was clear there was no hope for him and his writing, especially if he had to give up this apartment and go and live in some cheap and grungy basement bachelor unit, an intolerable scenario that conjured up old memories of agoraphobia and alcoholism, which he likened to "living like a rat."

Had Daniel succeeded in chasing me away right then and there, perhaps he would have killed himself a few weeks earlier than he actually did. I don't know. Regardless, our dynamic of caregiver and cared-for went on, with an inevitability that is easy to see now. Daniel's extreme pessimism struck me as over the top then, the depression talking in a particularly bad moment that would surely pass. And so I said what I thought was the only right thing to say, and meant it: "Daniel, I know these are really rough times, but it will get better. It has to. Regardless of what happens, you are my friend, I love you, and I'm not going to abandon you." This may not have been music to a suicidal man's ears, but I am glad I said it. There are few comforts for a suicide survivor, but knowing that I did my best while Daniel was alive, that I genuinely, if misguidedly, tried to help, that I didn't lash out or say something I would regret, has allowed me to live with myself a little more peacefully, after the raging chaos of emotion subsided.

Amid the dark memories are other, happier ones. I would stare at photos of Daniel taken at Christmas, and feel a sense of bewilderment. How could the man smiling in these pictures kill himself six weeks later? Here's Daniel grinning in my kitchen as he whips up mashed potatoes, while my father carves the turkey. Daniel in mock rapture as he savours one of the Harrods's truffles my sister has brought him from London as a gift. Daniel looking pleased with himself as he sits on the couch between me and Grainne. Throughout January, he, my roommates, and I would linger over dinner at my place, laughing and talking. There were nights out, seeing the odd second-run movie, enjoying a cheap meal out. There were good conversations, quiet moments. There was one disturbing temper meltdown on his part, the only time I ever saw him take out his anger and frustration by shouting at me, after which I told him I was worried about him. He apologized the next day. There was the time I retrieved my phone messages, and listened to a clip of unfamiliar music, puzzled at first, until I recognized the jaunty rhythms of Herb Alpert and the Tijuana Brass, from the album *Midnight Sun* that I'd bought Daniel for Christmas, after he surprised and amused me by saying he genuinely liked that music. This from a man more likely to collect the work of bands with names like the Lunachicks and Bunchoffuckingoofs, and to relax listening to gangsta rap—"last bastion of male anger," he had once observed, approvingly. There was no accompanying voice message. "So, you called for a reason?" I later asked him. "No, I was just thinking of you," he said, smiling. I had found his playfulness a sign that he was not as dangerously down as I had thought.

Back and forth, over and over the same ground, sometimes confirming your worst suspicions, long after the fact, goading yourself into asking how you could have been so stupid, and then turning around and seeing an instant replay of an altogether sunnier picture, one that absolves as much as it confuses you in all your usual points of reference and interpretation. How could he, when . . . ?

But he did. That is the fact, regardless of what you saw or didn't see, heard or didn't hear, said or didn't say, did or didn't do. None of it matters now, even though for a time you can't help rehearsing it.

He did.

April 1994. I'm back at the Palmerston Library, researching a story on hiking trails in Canada for *Equinox*. I walk down an aisle and am suddenly assailed by the memory of the last time I was here, the crazy dash to the phone booth, the strange conversation we had, my misplaced fear, now so dreadfully ironic, that Daniel's life was in danger due to a meal I'd served. Death by mozzarella. No, I needn't have worried, it wasn't going to happen that way, nor for that matter by way of an ancient chunk of smoked Gruyère. Another occasion when I find myself momentarily caught between laughter and tears.

My step goes leaden, I feel a familiar, instant sapping of energy, an I-don't-give-a-shit listlessness that makes working difficult. I try to force myself. However, I become so lost in memory and emotion, I am startled when I tune back in and realize where I am. Still in the earliest stages of grief, I am subject to these periodic zone-outs. Usually, they happen in the privacy of my office, when I am alone and can simply turn from my work and stare into space, or rest my head on my desk, or write something in my journal, or cry unseen and unheard. Usually that is enough to restore me to a functioning state. I have wondered how I would have managed in these first months if I had had to work in a more public space.

There is the first time an ambulance comes wailing down College Street, the siren's intrusive blare traveling up through my office window in the old building on the corner of Euclid, straight to the panic centre of my nervous system. It jolts me from my chair to pace and sob uncontrollably, images of fresh trauma and crisis imposing themselves onto my memories of February 14, a little farther down the street. When silence returns and I am calmer, I cannot settle. I feel lost, at odds, demolished. Finally, I turn off the lights and lie down on the floor, my eyes fixing on the strip of light coming from the hallway under the door. It's quite soothing really, lying here inert, staring out like an animal hidden in its burrow, the silence interspersed with the carpeted thud of feet passing by, making the floor vibrate a little, muffled voices filtering in. How long did I stay like that? I can't remember, but I do recall bracing myself for a long time after, whenever ambulances roared by. In downtown Toronto that was rather often.

Sirens couldn't be avoided, but College Street could be. For about a year, the stretch between Euclid and Grace was my own private nuclear-spill zone. I purposefully detoured around the area, even when it was extremely inconvenient. The first time I steeled myself and ventured into the Cafe Diplomatico about a year later, I felt a twinge of pain when one of the owners smiled at me in a kind of surprised where-have-you-been? recognition. *Please don't ask,* I thought to myself, and mercifully he didn't. Slowly, I reclaimed the ability to walk down the street, shop, meet friends; even finally and monumentally walk right past the apartment itself, stop in front of the building for a moment and acknowledge my terrible connection to it, and what happened there, without feeling overwhelmed.

All of what I describe are standard symptoms of grief in the first months after a traumatic loss. While knowing this can help a mourner feel less crazy, less isolated, it cannot truly console or make the powerful feelings subside. Months or years can pass before you can look back and place your behaviour in some kind of coherent pattern or context. In the very beginning, shock reduced me to help-lessness in my daily routines. I forgot to eat, lost any normal sleep pattern, and failed to perform the most basic of tasks competently. I once walked down the wrong street to a friend's house, a place I had visited dozens of times, turning off a main thoroughfare one street too soon. I actually got right to the door of the house situated one street over, and raised my hand to knock before realizing with a surge of confusion that this wasn't Laima's place.

I became irrationally frustrated when these things happened— *who the hell moved Laima's house anyway? Has this bank machine gone berserk? This* is *my* PIN *number! It's not? Oh. Sorry.* Frequently during those weeks, I lost my train of thought in the middle of conversations, felt a flash of shame: "Did I already tell you this?" Sometimes the answer was yes, sometimes no; always my friends were patient and understanding. Eventually, I acknowledged these upsetting mental lapses for what they were, normal symptoms of trauma, early precursors of the deep grief to follow. Now, when I hear of a suicide, I often observe a moment of silence not just for the deceased, but also for the survivors, who are now forgetting addresses and phone numbers and PINs, and who will stagger for weeks or months through a world gone strangely awry and out of their control.

And so, standing in the library on that April day, beset by a flurry of upsetting memories and feelings, my mind simply seizes up, and I revisit the panicky sense of losing control that marked my very first hours and days after Daniel's death. Blindly, I make my way to an aisle where no one else is standing. I have completely forgotten why I came here, what I am looking for. I don't want anyone to know how silly and confused I feel. I pull down a book, open it and rest it on the shelf, perusing it as though engrossed in the information there. My tears fall on colourful pages of photographs demonstrating golf swings. When I feel sufficiently composed, I close the book, walk out of the library, and go home. I spend the rest of the afternoon curled up on the couch.

Looking back on Daniel's suicide and its aftermath, I know I continued to function in a curious state of self-preserving denial, which lasted until well after the death had been confirmed beyond all doubt. Denial used to be considered a bad thing, and it can be, if someone gets stuck in it. I have met people who admitted that they shelved the grieving experience at the time of their loved one's suicide, in some cases not revisiting it for decades, even when they rationally accepted the death as real. In many cases of suicide, the seeds of this denial are planted long before the act itself is completed. Few suicides happen genuinely out of the blue. There are often signs and clues strewn along the survivor's backtracked path, making them ask themselves interminably, *Why didn't I see?* Some don't want to do that, at least not for a very long time, until they are at a safe distance from the event itself and able to separate themselves from guilt, blame, responsibility—feelings that may or may not be appropriate.

At best, unexperienced grief in the wake of a suicide lies deceptively dormant. In reality the feelings leap and prowl through an unexamined life in bouts of inexplicable anger, depression, anxiety, a panoply of addictions, faltering or broken relationships. At worst, denial can constitute a form of delusion, in which the unwilling mourner believes against all the evidence that the death was something other than a suicide—an accident, a murder, an incomprehensible act of God—or, bizarrely, that it did not occur at all.

93

Venal or merely obtuse outsiders may seek to capitalize on this kind of denial when it manifests on a mass scale. On a cold November night in 1996, I sat in a Toronto concert hall with a group of rapt young fans of Kurt Cobain, once the lead singer of the alternative grunge band Nirvana, who killed himself in 1994. They had come to hear the conspiracy theories being peddled by two journalists who have built a laughably shoddy case for suggesting that Cobain did not kill himself, but was the victim of a murder nefariously orchestrated by his wife, Courtney Love. Also in the audience that night were Love's legal representatives, flown all the way from L.A. and standing forbiddingly in their suits among the kids. The journalists delivered their gossipy goods, mainly based on the allegedly suspicious statements and actions of Love herself, and supported by, of all people, her superannuated hippie of a father, Hank Harrison, also present that evening to add his stale act to the exploitative circus. Courtney's daddy-o absurdly invoked the spirit of Neal Cassady, a crony of Jack Kerouac's who died decades ago, for a stunned young audience that had clearly never heard of him. Then, in what must go down as one of the most brilliant Freudian howlers of all time, he absolved himself of all responsibility for his daughter's teenage delinquency and other later personal difficulties by saying, "How could I have caused her problems, when after her mother and I divorced, I hardly ever saw her?"

The evening was a sorry spectacle. Classic denial after suicide, complicated by the fame factor, was laid bare in small, spurious details itemized in such a way as to suggest murder. The vastly greater weight of evidence pointing to suicide was oafishly misread or discounted.

Extreme cases aside, grief experts are now more inclined to view a certain degree of denial as a normal, healthy, even necessary part of any bereavement process. Initially, this reaction shields sufferers from the most life-threatening stress, so they can begin their march through the thick woods of grief toward accepting and integrating their loss. Just as a newly felled tree continues to nourish and support roots, so novice human mourners cannot in a moment absorb the enormous truth of a loved one's unexpected death. As I learned in the hardest way through losing Daniel, when we bond with others, they root deeply within us, and when they die, we discover just how intricately and integrally their roots have entwined with our own. For a while after the truth sinks in, the roots seem to scream in protest. Eventually their grip loosens, and they return to the grieving heart's soil, where the space made by a living person's presence is painfully transformed into enduring memory. We come to accept that these people who once shared our lives and then left us suddenly will never be as they once were. As we grieve, we learn to regard them, in our memories, with a more muted passion, though no less love. We sow the seeds for a new relationship with the dead. In this altered, yet no less profound way, they live on within us.

Still, it is a marvel how stubbornly reluctant we are to birth our griefs, to surrender to the hard labour, the searing pain of a traumatic loss such as a suicide. To do so means relinquishing all joy or happiness for a time. We must accept the past, present, and future as a project with new and unanticipated specifications, and one we may find an awkward design, a bad fit, a place we would never have imagined ourselves occupying and don't care to begin work on.

Our living attachments are exceedingly complex, kinetic, full of spark and energy, arcing and flexing through intricately constructed, subtly engineered, at times exquisite, private architectures, their points of connection seemingly infinite. When all is well, we dance confidently, gracefully, through our works of intimacy in progress, sure of our footing, and the solid foundations we trust are beneath us; we built them together, after all. To have to tear all this down before it's completed, to feel yourself crashing to the floor when your partner, whose rhythms are just beginning to run along smoothly with yours, suddenly drops you and disappears—it is hard to know what your next move should be, counterintuitive, wrong somehow, to have to dismantle this place you treasured and were coming to know so well.

Perhaps there are tough souls capable of instantly bringing in the wrecking ball, and watching it thoroughly demolish the whole edifice of a relationship without a flinch, sustaining barely a scratch on their hard hats. I suspect there are few with such nerves of steel. And few would care to go to the opposite, unhealthy extreme, taking up squatter's rights in the condemned structure and dancing alone through its empty rooms into eternity. There lurks always the gruesome spectre of Dickens's Miss Havisham, her life eerily stilled of its natural momentum in youth, her perpetually worn wedding gown mouldering as her own flesh decays, and she forever waits for the man that got away. What an electrifying human truth lies at the heart of this classic fictional portrayal, and how telling that one of the most memorable characters in English literature embodies the tragic state of eternally unresolved mourning.

Most of us are neither hard hat nor Havisham in our grief reactions, but we do need time to contemplate what we are losing before we are prepared to let it go, especially when the loss has been sudden. Exactly a month from the day I found Daniel dead, I wrote in my journal:

> I realize there is a part of me that does not want to let go of Daniel—that to "get over" my grief is to abandon him, a part of myself, the person I was, the hopes I had when he was alive. This is so hard. I know that in a way, I have not yet said good-bye to Daniel, that I can't yet, that I begin to cry at the thought, though I know it is inevitable . . . Still so much tenderness and longing in my thoughts about Daniel. Like lingering on the shore before pushing my boat away, never to return. Feel lost and utterly alone at the thought of this. Keep replaying things in my memory, knowing this won't change anything, or make death any less final.

Anyone who has suffered a major grief will recognize the feeling of being held by the past, in the very early days after a death. We want, *need,* to restore our bearings, reorient ourselves, walk through the familiar, now empty, rooms, gaze at the spaces. We need to imagine the past, perhaps rehearse a few of the remembered steps, for old times' sake, so that we have the courage to say goodbye, shut the door, and sail away for good with our memories: *Here's where this happened, and that reminds me of the time, and over here, wasn't this where . . .* There's no formula or strict schedule to follow, but somehow this work of ordering and placement, this fixing in memory must happen to enable the present and future to unfold and begin to have coherent meaning again. And work it most definitely is, though not the kind done nine-to-five, not the kind you clock in and out of, that comes with a handy job description. Given the demands of most people's lives, it's work that tends to get done when no one—perhaps even you—is looking, rather randomly and haphazardly, often under social pressures to integrate quickly and unobtrusively into normalcy and routine again.

In the initial stages of grief, it seems that literally every moment and every thought is infused with an awareness of the absent person and his or her death. You cannot expect to bypass the mourning process, so as not to pose embarrassment and discomfort to others at this point. Such a demand may feel as hopeless as trying to fit an ocean into a wading pool; it can't be done. Thankfully, I never felt such a push from friends or family, who were patient and compassionate when I was thoroughly immersed in sorrow. Even with all this support, I recall times when I worked and went about my business with a facade of normalcy in place, while silently screaming within.

The brittle and unyielding nature of day-to-day contemporary lives can make people in mourning feel even crazier and more lost. Over the past few decades, many have formed support groups to help themselves, whatever the source of their bereavement. The impulse to do so is understandable, and many people who would otherwise grieve silently and alone find immeasurable comfort in those Tuesday-night, church-basement circles that now exist in virtually every city of North America. Here their tears and bewilderment and anger are accepted and understood, and they may find themselves eventually strong enough to comfort someone else. Yet it is a sad comment that so many find that they cannot get this kind of support through their existing social networks. Until a setback such as a sudden death hits us full on, most of us are perhaps unaware of the degree to which our lives are structured as though by the design of an anal-retentive, nineteenth-century efficiency expert, called into the factory to maximize production. Throw in grief, and the assembly line of a modern individual's life is potentially pitched into disarray that may not be accepted or understood in his or her wider community. Those in mourning can feel isolated and marginalized. Others may skirt awkwardly around them, not sure what to say, ever watchful for signs that at last, the person is "back to normal." (Anyone with experience in bereavement will tell you that listening, and simply being there, is more helpful than saying the "right" things.) Most corporate bereavement-leaves fall far short of the time an employee may need to genuinely absorb the shock and be restored to "normal." A one-size-fits-all approach to mourning is bound to be of limited use; we must each grieve at our own pace and in our own way. Styles of grieving do differ dramatically, from culture to culture, family to family, and person to person.

In our homogenized, productivity-worshipping, secular society, the message seems to be that it would be best if grief didn't exist at all. If it must, we will grudgingly allow it a modicum of space in our lives. Such rituals as traditional days of the dead strike us as morbid, strange, even frightening. We prefer to write them off as quaint holdovers from primitive times that continue to exist in less developed countries only for the benefit of tourists. In reality, such sacred and ancient festivals that dwell deliberately for a defined period of time on our connection to and feeling for the dead are thoroughly healthy expressions of the most essential of human needs. If we allowed ourselves to channel our grief in this intense, contained way, we might actually resolve it sooner, and the dead could be integrated into our lives more seamlessly.

"I'm grievin' as fast as I can!" wrote one woman wryly, in an online support group forum for suicide survivors. She was describing how unreasonably pushed she felt when, only four months after her husband's suicide, a friend had pronounced that a pretty young woman like her shouldn't be alone, insisted she started dating again, and tried to set her up with a man she thought suitable. The grieving woman was horrified to be called upon to fulfill someone else's agenda for what was best for her. All she wanted to do, all she could do at this stage, was nurse her unhealed emotional wounds.

With this kind of pressure to cheer up or shut up, some mourners push themselves into an appearance of having healed, long before that is really the case. It's an expectation that also stems from a fundamental misunderstanding about the nature of grief and mourning. Grief isn't just about keening and wailing; it isn't primarily the hysterical gnashing of teeth and tearing of hair. It is a process, a long one, that involves much reflection, many quiet moments, and the time and space in which to digest one's whole loss. This takes years. While it may begin with all the stock images of grieving, it gradually becomes something far less obvious, though no less consuming. Victoria Alexander, author and editor of *Words I Never Thought To Speak*, herself a suicide survivor, suggests that for most people, the grieving process after a suicide may take seven to ten years to come full circle—to bring a mourner to a point where the suicide is no longer a central defining reference point in her life. This does not mean that mourners spend all those years in grief's full regalia; if they did, their condition would come under the category of "complicated mourning" and they would best be treated clinically. No, the initial post-suicide shock is only the stone hitting the water; it is the ever-so-gradually diminishing concentric circles of the inevitable ripples that suicide survivors are left to trace. With such a large stone, there are a lot of circles to follow, until the surface of the water is smooth again.

Regardless of one's circumstances, the tasks of grieving after a traumatic loss are often invisible, largely unconscious, and in the beginning, once the disorientation and Novacaine numbness of initial shock has worn off, tend to be done twenty-four hours a day. Before I experienced it myself, I didn't understand how *physical* grief over a sudden loss is, how instinctive, how deep in our bones, from the initial moment of shock on. During the first weeks after Daniel's death, I lay like a stillborn foal in my bed after nights of bad dreams, my arms stretched uselessly in front of me, feeling as though they had been ripped from their sockets. They literally ached, in a way that no amount of rubbing or favouring would alleviate. Later, I read that mothers who lose their infants often report this particular symptom. If the physically intimate relationship we share with a lover is analogous to the mother-infant bond, then it made sense to me: It was as though Daniel were an extension of my own body that had been violently wrenched away, and like an amputee suffering the phantom pain of a lost limb, I retained a body awareness that still yearned to encompass my absent other half.

I also noticed early on, while sitting curled up in a chair talking to a friend, that I had unconsciously taken on a gesture of Daniel's. Often, he would prop his elbow on a table or a chair arm and cup his hand over his skull, especially after he shaved his head, occasionally moving his fingers as though to massage his scalp, in an attitude of combined protection and weary concentration that reminded me of an old scholar or sage ruminating on some ancient philosophical problem. There I was, doing exactly the same thing. I don't know whether I had ever done this before Daniel's death, whether some of our physical habits had begun to transfer back and forth in shared familiarity. In some way, at that moment of recognition, it brought comfort. As with the aching limbs, I later read that taking on the deceased person's gestures and behaviour is not unknown in the first stages of grief.

Certainly in the first weeks, as the grief books also describe, I was, to put it mildly, preoccupied. From the moment I rose with my throbbing arms, I washed in Daniel water, read Daniel in the newspaper, put him on with my coat, and breathed him in with the cold morning air. *Daniel's dead, Daniel's dead, Daniel's dead,* went some relentless engine in my head as I stepped heavily along the street each day to my office. I lived in the oversized black turtleneck I had given Daniel for Christmas. Entries for March and April in the journal I kept reflect my mental state. "Desolation . . . there is no other word . . . I feel a horrible brokenness . . . lost, hopeless . . . comforting myself with thoughts of him near me, while knowing I'll never see, feel, touch him again . . . the comfort his presence brought me that I can't find now . . . angry at people for all the ways they are not Daniel."

For months, I experienced a vivid, surreal world through heightened senses rubbed raw. I had little interest in reading anything except poetry; I wanted my truths straight up, to hell with the slower, watered-down effect of sentences and paragraphs. Permanently primed for intensity, ever alert for fresh onslaughts of huge emotion, I found a way to make everything I perceived connect in some way to Daniel's death. It must have been May, because I recall the tulips and irises swaying brightly as I walked down Palmerston Avenue, past all the huge, impressive old houses with their lovingly tended gardens out front. A stooped old woman looked up from sweeping her walkway and smiled tooth-lessly at me. A woman about my age walked by with a little girl skipping beside her, sweet and lovely in a soft blue velvet tam. A group of teenage schoolgirls trooped by in their uniforms, all glossy hair, smooth, lean limbs, and lusty lungs, boisterously loud and with no idea that they should do anything other than take up all the space they wanted, their nonchalant perfection breathtak-ing. A thin, bent old man in a tweed cap and long coat shuffled slowly along with a cane some distance behind them. I wanted to stop in the middle of all this life unfolding as it should and shout, *Why is that you are alive and Daniel is not? Why is it that I am alive and Daniel is not?* My outrage was blindly selfish, urgent—I wanted Daniel to be alive, and right then, so I could savour and delight in him the way I did all these other living creatures, whose lives were surely no more important and worth celebrating than his. I suppose in my rage I was even arrogant enough to imagine they were less so.

Another strangely physical phenomenon that often occurs during acute grief is imagining that you see the deceased alive—and everywhere. It can be shocking. Once, when sitting with a friend in a long, narrow, dimly lit restaurant, I saw approaching in the distance along the aisle . . . Daniel! Had to be him. Same walk, same long legs, same fair complexion, big eyes, bald head. I sat transfixed, somehow resisting the impulse to rise from my chair and run to him in some farcical, slow-motion, "Thank God you're alive, darling!" reunion. I sat speechlessly trying to maintain my composure, as the young man began wiping down the table beside us, and I saw it wasn't Daniel at all. After regarding my reaction to the resembalnce without comment, my friend silently studied the menu, slapped it shut, and briskly suggested we order some wine.

Yes, I saw him walking down the street, passing in cars, stepping onto elevators, leaving doctors' offices; it is not just Elvis who never really died and now wanders the doughnut shops of the world. It is as though all the psychological wiring that once found precise connection on the unique planes and contours of your loved one's face now flails wildly in search of any reasonable facsimile set of features on which to alight and fasten. Maybe all this unconscious seeking and finding of the deceased is indeed a matter of brain circuitry. The ability to recognize familiar faces is a cognitive tool honed from earliest infancy, so basic to our natures that we take it for granted. A rare neurological condition impairs this essential life skill. In grief, it is as though the reverse happens:

Your ability to recognize one particular face shifts into hypersensitive overdrive. Not just faces either, of course, but gaits, tones of voice, and gestures. I wasn't the only one to experience this; even Daniel's psychiatrist admitted to me in a touching letter that he had on occasion seen Daniel in the street himself.

When it happened to me, in the beginning anyway, I felt as if I had regressed to the primitively reasoning creature I'd become in the initial moments of shock after finding Daniel: a childlike bargainer, arguing against all known laws of the physical universe. Here was tall, bald-headed Daniel, loping toward me along the street, or in a restaurant, and suddenly half of me is thinking with an idiot hope my other half knows is pathetic: *Maybe he isn't dead after all! What if . . . I mean, what if???? Maybe he faked it, maybe he crawled out the window, managed somehow to lock it from the inside, left behind some kind of doppelganger stand-in that managed to fool a dozen police officers, four paramedics, and a team of coroners, so that he could begin a new life as a waiter at La Hacienda on Queen Street. I mean, maybe it could happen, maybe it just could!*

Yes, well, call in agents Mulder and Scully on your own personal X-file. Invariably, your theory is blown, as the person comes closer and reveals beyond all doubt that he is not who you thought he was. Yet even irrefutable evidence doesn't stop the search. I don't know how many Daniel sightings I've had over the past five years. Probably dozens, though they are now rare. Where I would once become upset, I now only smile when I see a tall, fair-skinned young man with a certain stirring resemblance and Danielesque demeanour—a good thing too, since the shaved-head look came back into vogue, and it seemed for a time that Daniels were popping up everywhere. Inwardly, I blow each one a kiss and wish him well.

Perhaps more than any other, this aspect of grief highlights the gulf between our emotional and our rational selves, a gulf that widens and deepens as we suffer; or maybe it is simply that, at these times, we are suddenly thrown off balance when our emotions come to the fore and take over. What a shock to be so felled by your own humanity, your own utter fallibility. To be taken in by these tricks of my own spirit was somehow a blow to my pride. At times throughout these months I felt like nothing so much as a painfully exhausted marathon runner, wishing I could plead with my crazily driven coach to let me stop because I had lost my own sense of purpose and didn't care to go on.

Above all else, there were tears, so many for a time that I angrily wanted to ask whatever God or gods exist whether there shouldn't be a statute of limitations on the number of tears one human being can cry in a lifetime. Why do some people get out of this life having cried perhaps a few spoonfuls, while others of us produce the equivalent of several brimming cisterns?

I cried standing at my dresser, picking up the dusky-blue lapis earrings Daniel had given me, along with a matching necklace of beaded thread, with an elegantly cut lapis pendant hanging from it, wafer-thin and subtly veined with meandering trails of soft gold, smooth on its surface, rough around the edges. A gift beyond Daniel's means, offered not for an occasion, but just because he wanted to give it. Where did this wild generosity of his come from, the same largesse that prompted him to buy lunches for people who were in worse financial shape than he was, or sometimes even when they weren't? It was only one of many gifts that Daniel gave me in our short time together, until I had to ask him to stop, because charming as it was, he really couldn't afford it.

I cried sitting on the sofa reading a newspaper obituary for poet Charles Bukowski; the old boozer who transformed his adventures in liver destruction into numerous poems and stories, as well as the screenplay of the film *Barfly*, had outlived Daniel by a month. Daniel and I had gone to see a play based on Bukowski's prose one night when we were just getting to know each other. I had laughed to myself when Daniel had suggested going along to something called *Erections, Ejaculations, Exhibitions,* produced by a Vancouver fringe theatre company called The Way Off Broadway Group and performed in a tiny theatre space at the corner of Dovercourt and Queen. We both found the play engaging, if bizarre. For all his confusions about women, there is something bullishly honest and humane about Bukowski's comical, chagrined view of the world. I had thought it propitious that Daniel and I both laughed at one point when no one else did, and later sat silent as others around us reacted with amusement to some gag or other that left us unmoved.

I cried when I passed the fruit and vegetable market, because I remembered the moment I had been fleetingly terrified of Daniel's vulnerability. I cried because I had shoved the thought away, and because the apricots brimming from bins outside reminded me of those tender, perfect apricots he held out to me the first time he had stood on my doorstep.

I cried in the living room on the first grey day of spring, Daniel's birthday. While it rained from morning until night, I lit a fire and listened to his favourite tape, Pablo Casals playing Bach.

I cried at my desk, a month after Daniel's death, writing a card to congratulate a friend on the arrival of her infant son, named Isaac. "He laugheth" she had written on the birth announcement. *Oh Isaac,* I thought to myself as I wrote, *I hope that is so for the rest of your life.*

I cried picking at the wood grain on the chair where Daniel had sat year after year in his psychiatrist's office. I stared at the pattern in the carpet as the doctor said to me firmly, kindly, "You are not responsible for his death." I didn't yet quite believe it.

I cried in my father's backyard on an overcast summer day, drinking a cup of tea he had made for me, as I looked out at the steel-grey waves of Lake Ontario. Behind me in the house, I could feel my father hovering awkwardly, looking out the window at the lake too. "I wish there was something I could do," he had said to me shortly after he had heard the news. I had no way then to guide him or anyone else, and I still didn't months later, sitting there alone in the yard where my father had taken pictures of Daniel and me standing together beside one of the flowering mock orange

bushes the summer before, pictures discreetly tucked out of sight
by this following summer. I guess he had found something he
could do. It must have been difficult for my father to comprehend.
He had lost his wife of forty-seven years, my mother, less than three
years earlier. He was only now really adjusting to his own life as a
widower. He had liked Daniel, even ventured to read one of his
chapbooks, one I thought relatively safe for a member of the older
generation to tackle, *The Job After the One Before*. It described a
young man's ill-fated attempts at gainful employment after being
sprung from a mental ward, and culminated in a furiously funny
climax in which the protagonist is dumped into a mailbox with a
stream of letters. My father said he thought it was good, that
Daniel's pared-down writing style reminded him of Hemingway.
He said he thought he understood some of what Daniel must have
been feeling—the financial stress, the professional disappointment.
Still, he said, it was hard to understand, wasn't it?

Yes, it was. Still.

And I cried many times at my computer, writing words that I
still did not want to believe Daniel would never read.

When not crying, I spent many moments in a state of stunned
suspension. I remember being alarmed once at my reflection in the
bathroom mirror, after some reminder or another had thrown me
off guard, wondering if I would ever get that smashed-up look off
my face. Or standing spooked in the darkened upstairs hallway
wrapped in a towel, my hair wet from a shower, caught between
rooms, my house-mate having put on John Coltrane playing "My
Favorite Things" as background music. She sat quietly working on
an essay at the dining room table, not knowing how it would twist
me up as I remembered Daniel, our bodies, exhausted, wanting for
nothing together on the previous summer's hottest night, that
song dancing over us, dense and pungent as a tropical wind.

One evening, my friends rented the movie *Breakfast At Tiffany's*.
Something about the George Peppard character lying in bed smoking, his languid writerly depression, his cynical resignation, his

redeeming tenderness, reminded me so much of Daniel that I felt a panicky, trapped sense of sadness. This grief at its heaviest, most oppressive, and inescapable wasn't something I felt I could share with my friends, who were nibbling popcorn and simply enjoying the campy, nostalgic film. I sat sweating in silence, with what must have been a weird, tight smile on my face, my eyes burning with unshed tears, and I kept thinking, *Daniel, my poor dead man, I will never forget that it was, of all things, "Moon River" I caught you humming in the bathtub that time. That's the memory that burst out the first time I poured apple gel in a bath after you died, the image of you rising like a genie on the fragrant scent, lying there so peacefully, your long legs crossed at the ankles and resting up the wall. "Such a nihilist," I had teased, and you had looked up from the bubbles. I don't think you even knew you had been humming out loud. Or what you were revealing. You just smiled and kept on humming. And now I can hardly endure thinking of it, sitting here on an ordinary Saturday night, watching a video with friends, pretending things can be normal even though you are dead, and dying myself a little inside.*

And then, anger.

Oh, *that.* In the beginning, right after Daniel's death, I was too destroyed by the sense of shock and loss to feel it. The first book I read as I tried to understand what was happening to me was *Silent Grief: Living in the Wake of Suicide,* by Christopher Lukas, a suicide survivor, and Henry M. Seiden, a psychologist. I read the considerable portions of the book devoted to anger—in particular, anger at the deceased—with a sense of detached curiosity. I could relate to the descriptions of trauma, the bargaining, the denial, the waves of emotional response, including guilt, anxiety, blame, anger at others and at myself. I could voraciously digest their advice that "instead of being passive victims of their fate, survivors can make accommodations and can respond to their fate; they can become active in their own behalf and active in their own lives . . . we are talking about the use of as many parts of the survivor's being as possible, about becoming unstuck, about continuing a process in which the survivor is a participant, not an observer. Responding, not reacting." But be angry at poor, defeated, dead Daniel? I couldn't imagine it. In fact, the book's authors emphasized the importance of this kind of anger so strongly that I tried to feel it, as if conscientiously doing some kind of self-improving mental exercise. I soon realized it was pointless. You either feel something or you don't. I couldn't manufacture anger just because some grief experts thought I should.

Gradually I did begin to ask myself why it was that I did not feel this rather key emotion. I met someone I had not seen in a long while on a bus shortly after Daniel's death, at a point when I was still looking and feeling haunted. She had heard about the suicide, though obviously didn't know many of the details. I was shocked when, after expressing concern for me, she contemptuously called Daniel an asshole. While she meant it supportively, I suppose, I wasn't in any shape to hear such bluntly expressed judgments, and felt myself shrinking back, still protecting Daniel, his retreat from the cruel world. A male friend had called in the days after the death, his voice sounding gravelly, as if he'd been crying. But I heard an unyielding coldness and anger when he said the first thing he had thought when he heard the news was what a jerk Daniel was to have done this to me. All I could think at the time was, *Done this to me? But he is the one who is dead!* In those early days, I see now that I spent a lot of time deflecting other people's anger toward Daniel and suppressing my own. Other people had less at stake in expressing it.

I did come to see that that was how it was. My anger was indeed there, but I was pushing it to one side, allowing the larger, predominantly sorrowful thoughts and feelings to deluge forth as they had to. As early as March 1994, I wrote in my journal that I was "starting to feel some anger," though I then added "maybe." Now I can recall what I could not risk admitting then: that for a moment, as I stood in Daniel's apartment, legs trembling, heart pounding, shouting, and vainly knocking on that locked door, barely able to accept what the terse contents of the little note tacked to it meant, I did rebuke him: *You have no right to place your life in my hands,* is I believe how it went. So I had had the self-protective wherewithal to at least think it, before burying it away for several years, before it seemed safe to allow it to surface again.

And now, at a distance of years, it doesn't seem such a bad thought. I've always felt that the notion of "rights" applied to suicide is meaningless—regardless of whether people, or those around them, believe they have a "right" to kill themselves, legally, morally, or spiritually, people will do it if they feel compelled to do so. Insofar as all adults capable of reason are responsible for their own behaviour and its impact on others, I must have felt in some visceral way that Daniel, for all the pain he bore, had trespassed against me; that it would take some time for me to truly and whole-heartedly forgive; that in fashioning a life-or-death situation whose outcome depended in part on the chance that I might come upon the note on the locked door before it was too late, he had placed a burden of responsibility on me that I had not known was there, and that I did not feel I deserved to carry. This was especially true when, having failed to stop his death-in-progress, by an unbearably thin margin, that burden of responsibility rolled heavily over into an even bigger burden of guilt.

Daniel's death hurt many people. I would not presume to guess how these people, in their own hearts, interpret his act through their own unique relationships with him. Though Daniel expressed his regrets, this act of placing me on the freshly scorched earth—the only person, had I known, likely to have stumbled in a little sooner and have thus altered the course of our lives—stuck with me for a long time. You have got to have a little anger in your heart for someone who does that to you, even if he didn't mean to, even if he felt sorry for doing it, even if—especially if—he is dead. It has taken years to be able to articulate the primary, specific, root cause of this particular anger.

The anger I did feel was first turned against others, toward myself, toward the whole, terrible, hopelessly flawed human reality that had been so trying for someone like Daniel to navigate. It is common for suicide survivors to feel this way toward people who have killed themselves, who may seem in the wake of their deaths to be pure victims of circumstance, brilliant, beleaguered souls brought down by a world too brutishly stupid to appreciate their extraordinary gifts. Often what makes artists so acutely visionary and sensitive to beauty also makes them keenly susceptible to pain, the human equivalents of those ferns that curl inward at the merest brush of a passing creature. In some ways, Daniel felt life that deeply, and suffered for it, like all those others simultaneously blessed and cursed.

But compassion for the dead is one thing; deification is another. While I could feel the former, I knew I had to beware of the latter, in order to truly heal myself and restore my life to its own bearings. Inevitably, the anger I felt toward others finally served as the conduit for my anger toward Daniel. Months after his suicide, it rolled in on a dramatic summer rainstorm, and lashed out of me finally with the sheer and abrupt force of the thunder and lightning that flashed through and rattled the windows of the room I was sitting in.

It was, all too appropriately, a dark and stormy night, the downpour finally erupting from the preceding stillness of the kind of heavily humid day in which everything and everyone seems to be lying low, in wait for something to give, burst forth, bringing some relief from the clammy heat. I was alone in the house, staring at various legal papers, documents, and manuscripts, the distasteful detritus of Daniel's death, spread out before me on the dining room table, as appealing as the yearly tax chore. I had to draft some letter or other to some lawyer or other. I sat there, reluctant to deal with it all again, contemplating all the ugly, hurtful things that had been done and said in the six months since February, the misery this suicide had brought into several lives. The cliché that death reveals the best and the worst in people happens to be true. I hated some of the behaviour I'd witnessed, hated that I'd been exposed to it, felt crushed by the cruelties, petty and large, heed-lessly meted out. It amazed me that people didn't see the absurdity of pointing fingers at another one for not seeing the obvious; if Daniel had been so clearly suicidal, why had they failed to prevent it from happening themselves? I was beating myself up enough anyway to make further blows somehow redundant. I hadn't asked for this, none of us in the maelstrom had, but I couldn't write myself out of the biography, even if others might have found it emotionally preferable if I had.

I'm not sure which was worse, other people's efforts to airbrush me out of Daniel's personal history, or when that failed, to demean the relationship we'd had. The underlying motive—to question the nature and depth of my grief over the loss—stunned me. The attitude struck me as going against some fundamental truth—that a person can affect us profoundly in the space of moments; quality and kind of relationship determine the nature of grief felt after a death. I wasn't interested in questioning other people's grief over the loss of Daniel; I found myself fiercely on the defensive when I felt others trying to discount mine. As I read later, the bereaved often tussle for the thorny crown of Designated Mourner, especially after a suicide, as though it is such a prize, as though there could be, with rare exceptions, only one. "For some-one who was so organized, he left quite a mess behind," observed the estate court judge who eventually validated Daniel's suicide note as his legitimate last wishes. She was painfully right.

As I sat and reflected on all of this, it suddenly seemed so daunt-ing, so oppressive, so pointless. As I stared out at the bushes whip-ping around in the wind, their delicate clusters of creamy flowers being pounded by the heavy rain, I felt seized with a white-hot anger. "You fucking bastard," I believe I hissed out loud. I pounded my fist against the table, stood up and sent the entire pile of papers flying across the room with an impulsive sweep of my arm. I rampaged around the room, wanting to shout at the ghost of Daniel, "You were *loved!* How could you do this, when so many people cared about you? How selfish of you to just throw your life away and leave the rest of us to clean up after it! How dare you show such contempt for the love freely offered to you!"

I felt better almost immediately. Cleansed, unclogged, as though my emotional path had been cleared of annoying, useless scrub in this frenzy. Now I could catch my breath and walk calmly on. I did feel anger at Daniel again, but never of the same magnitude. Perhaps after this catharsis, I could accept that it was there, that it might leap forth again, along with other emotions, but it didn't have to overwhelm me, and I didn't have to keep it at bay. I was getting a little closer to accepting the ups and downs that characterize grief, the unpredictable waves of emotion that with time, you learn to accommodate, until finally it feels once again that you, not your raw emotions, are the one driving.

To sustain anger at the person long gone would only compound the tragedy. As necessary as those moments of fury at Daniel were, they could not dominate the way I felt and thought. I needed to heal, however slowly. Just as I knew that Daniel was loved, I also understood the reasons why it had been easy for him to forget that. Just as I knew that the outcome of Daniel's act might be judged as selfish in what it took from others emotionally, I know that for most suicidal people, the last thing their act is is selfish.

This notion of the person's selfishness is one of the most persistently aired and least examined views of suicide. It's rooted in the natural emotion of anger, but it's an inadequate base for any coherent analysis of a suicidal person. At the point when many people seek to eradicate themselves, they have the lowest self-esteem imaginable. They may well feel they are, in some fundamental way, already dead; the final, suicidal act may seem a mere formality to a person in that state. Choosing to live, for any one of us, is in many ways a far more selfish thing to do. It requires robust self-esteem to pull off a life well-lived, bold self-assertion, and an unapologetic sense of entitlement to breathe air, take up space, and fashion an existence we believe has meaning to ourselves and to others. If suicidal people could imagine that for themselves, they'd be laughing. And living.

No, maintaining a sense of moral superiority over suicidal people is misplaced, even cruel. If you have never experienced suicidal feelings yourself, and view with incomprehension anyone who does, consider yourself lucky, not superior. Victims of chronic and severe forms of mental illness such as schizophrenia and manic depression, for example, come by their suicidal impulses genetically; neither they nor their families can be considered guilty of any moral failing. In many cases, expecting someone to simply buck up and conquer suicidal feelings is like asking a man with two broken legs to skate in the NHL. Indeed, former star hockey player Sheldon Kennedy might never have left the ice if he hadn't been kneecapped into depressive despair by his early experiences in life. He suffered sexual abuse and intimidation at the hands of a sadistic minor league coach throughout his teen years. Now Kennedy, in his early thirties, devotes much of his time to campaigning for greater public awareness about child abuse, and is raising funds to build a ranch in the Rockies for children scarred by abuse. "Suicide was a happy thought for me from the moment [the abuse] happened until it ended," Kennedy admits. In speaking publicly and without shame about his past, Kennedy provides an unusual role model for men, and could do more to reduce suicide rates than a raft of psychiatrists and drug manufacturers. Owing to his age, sex, and history of abuse and subsequent depression, he stands in a high-risk group for suicide, and simultaneously among those least likely to speak openly about their emotional difficulties and seek help. In one radio interview in the summer of 1998, when Kennedy was rollerblading across Canada in his crusade to build his ranch and raise awareness about child abuse, he recounted how a well-dressed man with an expensive car approached him and told him haltingly that he, too, had been abused. Then he began "crying like a baby," in Kennedy's words. "I was the first person he ever told," he continued, incredulously.

Perhaps things are changing for the better, for men. "Now we're patted on the back for speaking out, but we used to be considered weirdos or losers," Kennedy reflected. Still, it takes guts for a man to do this; by going against the macho grain, Kennedy reveals genuine strength. Yet he also admits that battling his emotional difficulties is an ongoing struggle, with potential setbacks.

Others are not so lucky. Martin Kruze was one of many young men sexually abused as a boy by staff at Toronto's Maple Leaf Gardens hockey arena. Shortly before he killed himself in 1997, he had gone public with his story. A flood of similar allegations followed his courageous act from men he had emboldened to step forward after years of silence. Kruze rocketed from complete obscurity to a guest appearance on *Oprah* and many other talk shows in Canada and the United States in a matter of weeks, as had Sheldon Kennedy. But it seemed the psychologically damaged Kruze was unable to withstand the taxing demands of sudden fame. Or perhaps he had expected the limelight would at last sweep away his private darkness for good. When it didn't, and on a day when he was unable to secure a bed in a psychiatric ward, he walked to Toronto's infamous Bloor Viaduct, as he had on previous occasions, and this time jumped. His grieving family continued his campaign to help victims of childhood sexual abuse, and have gained Maple Leaf Gardens' financial support for a clinic to serve these abuse survivors.

Not long after Kruze's death, Toronto's Bloor Viaduct was in the headlines again, after a young student at a Roman Catholic boys' school jumped to his death, apparently in fear of being disciplined along with several other boys over a yearbook prank involving stories of alleged abuse from some staff members. An inquest followed to determine what had led to the boy's death; it was suggested, among other things, that the news coverage of Martin Kruze's suicide jump may have planted the seed of the idea in the boy's mind. This and other incidents caused much general public consternation over what to do about the alarming increase in the numbers of jumpers from the architecturally splendid yet lethally alluring viaduct. Eventually, it was decided that boundaries should be erected, though this struck some people as absurd. At a time when services for the mentally ill were being severely disrupted and in some cases eliminated, it was surely no surprise that more than the usual number of troubled souls were trailing away from the hospitals that no longer had room for them, to deal with their problems in the only way they thought was left. Now, said some wryly, the poor and desperate wouldn't even be allowed that last-ditch exit from their pain. Many suggested that rather than boarding up lovely old gems of Victorian engineering and design, the powers that be should reinstate the essential mental health services they were mistakenly treating as trimmable frills.

That and other debates continue. In the years after Daniel's death, I have found myself fascinated by the differing public reactions to various high-profile suicides. I am curious about my own, often contradictory thoughts and feelings as well. While the judgmental, sometimes simply ignorant tone of some coverage bothers me, I have come to appreciate that it is impossible to expect people, including me, not to make at least some judgments in the wake of a suicide. Just as we feel differently about a sadistic serial killer than we would about a battered wife who kills her husband after years of abuse, so we cannot help discerning the mitigating circumstances, or lack of them, in various suicides. Who could regard an aboriginal teenager who hangs himself after a life of abuse in a string of inadequate foster homes as anything but a blameless victim? Perhaps Martin Kruze had his obnoxious, demanding, manipulative side; still, knowing what he had been through, most felt only sorrow after his death.

BRITISH TEEN TAKES FATAL OVERDOSE AFTER 'FATTY' TAUNTS, ran the headline of another tragic story. "Neighbours said a gang of up to 15 youths gathered outside the family's house for several consecutive nights . . . They attacked the home several times, throwing a block of margarine through the window, shouting abuse about lard and fat, and calling her 'smelly,'" the sad report elaborated. Whatever psychological difficulties or family problems the girl suffered before the bullying (and later evidence said there were some), it would be unreasonable to suggest that the severe taunting of her peers was not a key factor in her decision to end her life. The link between extreme bullying and suicide is now being formally explored by psychologists. Regrettably, it is a common phenomenon.

Stories of deaths like these horrify us. We instinctively want to avenge them. Yet, how much more complex are our reactions to news of men (and sometimes, but rarely, women) who kill their families before killing themselves. Suddenly, we don't care what they may have suffered, what rendered them "poor copers," in the professional parlance, what brought them to the point of being capable of such heinous deeds. We flock to the funerals of their victims in droves, mourning their loss, their innocence; we bury the suicides quietly and grudgingly, with cursory eulogies heard by few in attendance. We would, it seems, rather condemn than understand, keeping our anger and incomprehension fresh for the next time it happens, rather than attempting to figure out why it happened at all, and how to make sure there is no next time. Suddenly, we are thrown back to the medieval past, when suicides were unconscionable felons, their bodies mutilated and left in the road for all to contemplate in horror.

Most media claim to be sensitive to the issue of suicide. They usually have some sort of official policy regarding how, or even whether, they will report instances of it. Despite this, I see inaccurate, incomplete, misleading, and sensationalist treatments and commonly held misconceptions about these deaths all the time. DISCO DUDS LED TO SUICIDE OF PUB MANAGER, INQUEST HEARS, went the headline of a 1998 story reprinted from England's *Daily Telegraph* in *The Ottawa Citizen*. One wonders why this, of all stories about suicide that must cross an editor's desk, deserved international play, except to give readers in Canada's capital a little chuckle with their morning coffee. My own unimpressed reaction was: "I somehow doubt it." As experts state repeatedly, the causes in any individual case of suicide are "multi-factoral"—perhaps in this thirty-nine-year-old man's case, being forced to wear "flared pants and a wig" did drive him to despair. Yet I am sure the story is infinitely more complicated than that. Had this pub manager been drinking or using drugs at the time? Had he ever suffered depression or attempted suicide in the past? What led to the breakup of his marriage? His exwife's testimony was reported exclusively in the thirty-seven-line-story. In presenting a simple, and indeed humorous, cause-and-effect story, the newspaper promoted a clichéd and inaccurate view of suicide. Cheap thrills, indeed.

Despite the steadily swelling annals of the discipline of suicidology, most people still hold often wildly contradictory views of suicide, sometimes even when looking at one and the same suicide. It's called a cowardly cop-out, or an act of bravery to be admired in some silent, backhanded way; a cry for help or a selfish affront; the easy way out, or the hardest decision a person could ever make; a sin, a sacrifice; egoistic, altruistic; an act of pure insanity, an act of supreme rationality; something that can and must be understood, painstakingly reconstructed by means of a "psychological autopsy"; something that doesn't and never will make any sense, no matter how you pull it apart and put it back together again. All, or none, of the above.

Nothing changes your perceptions of suicide like being near one. I thought that having been scarred this way, I would always be unreservedly sad toward any news of other poor souls who had succeeded in "completing" their suicides. In most cases I was. I felt a grim sorrow when it was announced that Mervin Goodeagle, a 19-year-old native actor on the CBC television drama *North of 60,* had hanged himself. I imagined the impact of his death on his family and community, on the cast of the program, and all on the native people, especially young ones, who looked to the show with pride. I imagined the heavy responsibility those involved with the program would feel, in the wake of such a high-profile young person's suicide, toward those communities, where life is sometimes

unbearable and suicide so prevalent. I wondered how the programmers would ultimately handle the news of the loss, given the
important consideration of the suicide "contagion effect" to which
young people are particularly vulnerable.* They handled it well,
with understated dignity, running at the end of one episode a
montage of scenes featuring the young actor, showing his name and
birth and death dates briefly, with sombre background music. The
message seemed right, a respectful good-bye that did not glorify the
suicide.

Some time later, I heard on the radio news that the actor
Graham Greene was in hospital under a suicide watch, after he'd
holed up in his house with a gun, threatening suicide, engaging the
police in a standoff. In what I've often thought was a ludicrously
inadequate media buzz-phrase, the news announcer stated gravely
that Greene had been "despondent over family matters." No doubt.
Most people who barricade themselves in their houses with guns
probably have been despondent about something, family matters
being one of the usual suspects. But I was shocked, actually saying
out loud to the radio, "No, you can't!"

As in, no, *you* can't. Greene, an enormously gifted actor in both

---

* When the Hobbema native reserves in Alberta experienced a dramatic increase in
youth suicides in the 1980s, elders and other counsellors discovered that the
teenagers had wrongly grasped a traditional teaching that when a person dies
before his time, he wanders lost in the spirit world. Several young people who had
survived suicide attempts said that after young friends of theirs had killed themselves, they had decided to go too, so that the other person wouldn't have to be
alone. Non-native specialists had failed to understand the meaning of this, but
once it was revealed to the elders, they were able to clarify for the young people
that it didn't work that way; if they died before their time, they too would wander
alone. This elder-based counselling, along with a massive and concerted community initiative, brought the suicide rate on the reserve down to almost zero in the
early 1990s. But gradual erosion of programs saw the rate creep up again. Today,
on many native reserves, the suicide rate, especially among young people, remains
catastrophic. Speaking to an audience of aboriginal youth in 1997, Phil Fontaine,
Grand Chief of The Assembly of First Nations, acknowledged, "There isn't one
aboriginal family that hasn't been affected by suicide."

comedy and drama, was one of the first native performers to make it to the big screen in roles that would have at one time been played by white people in makeup, new roles that went beyond insulting stereotypes, and might not even have existed before, on which Greene could put his own personal stamp. It may be true, as the old poem goes, that "each man's death diminishes me," but it seemed as I absorbed the news that there were some deaths by suicide the world could less afford than others, and surely this was one of them. It perhaps shouldn't really be a surprise to learn that such a unique and talented person is human, living a life filled with dilemmas and conflicts of a kind that might strain anyone to his emotional limits. Months later, seeing a full-page newspaper ad featuring Greene spiffed up in tailored duds, courtesy of Toronto clothier Harry Rosen, for a day of being Graham Greene—the public Graham Greene anyway—I felt curiously relieved, as though all was right with the world, so long as Graham Greene was not despondent over family matters.

I think about what Rabbi David Marmur said about suicide, when I interviewed him in his office at Holy Blossom Temple in Toronto. He spoke of the Jewish belief that each life is a gift from God, one to be cherished, lived to its fullest. In some sense, he told me, faithful human beings are "prisoners of hope." And if one of those prisoners of hope makes a jail break, is there room for forgiveness? I wanted to know. "Yes, yes, of course, forgiveness, there must always be forgiveness!" Marmur replied with passion. He told me of a brilliant colleague and neighbour he had had while living in England in the 1950s, a man of huge intellect and learning, and also of crippling paranoid delusions that medical knowledge at the time could not successfully treat. When he killed himself, it was a terrible loss, but also there was relief, to imagine that the man would not suffer anymore. Yes, I thought, leaving the rabbi's office, we all have our stories surrounding suicide, all have our ways of seeing it. Prisoners of hope. I liked that.

I thought I had no trouble accepting such a lesson—kind,

forgiving me. Then my feelings were tested when I read of the suicide in February 1997 of fifty-nine-year-old Jack Hickman, "merchant banker, corporate ethics reformer, alleged fraud artist," as one newspaper obituary described him. I first read of him in a profile of a flashy young society matron in *Toronto Life* magazine only three months earlier. Katherine Govier's article, "Surviving Harvey," documented the life of Pia Southam since the suicide of her wealthy scion husband, Harvey Southam, in 1991. Following that, she had married Hickman, a move that her friends considered hasty and ill-advised. She explained: "He lifted me out of my blahs. He had no fear of my situation and what I'd been through . . . We'd listen to Lakmé at volume five at four a.m . . . I began to feel liberated . . . ." She told Govier this before Hickman's suicide.

I winced. When I read Southam's rationalizations of what the dapper Hickman offered her, I understood them. I too, had become involved with someone before I was really finished with my own grieving, perhaps hoping against hope that there could be an easy exit from all the pain. It had been predictably short-lived. *Ah yes,* I thought as I read the *Toronto Life* piece, *Lakmé in the darkness before dawn.* I could just imagine how Southam must have seen it.

But while Lakmé provided the music of the night, it was "Hit the Road, Jack" at high noon. The harsher light of day and a couple of years of difficult relations revealed Hickman as a troubled man with questionable financial dealings in his past. Some apparently saw it coming, and indeed there was an uncomfortable foreboding embedded in Govier's piece, but Hickman's suicide by carbon monoxide poisoning in an old Rolls-Royce that belonged to Southam stunned many.

Reading his obituary, I was taken aback by the emotion I felt. Three years after Daniel's death, I thought I was beyond judging the unfortunate dead, especially those I didn't know. Evidently not. For the first time, my first and foremost response to a suicide was pure anger at the deceased. *Creep!* I thought to myself. *Fifty-nine-years-old, living a materially privileged existence, fancying your-*

self the big heroic savior of a widow and her two children, and now look what you have done! After everything they had been through! You ought to have known better than to pull such an evil stunt. How could you be so selfish? Yes, I unabashedly applied the S-word I so hated to hear others use.

Later, I ranted all this to a friend, someone who, as I recalled, had been inclined to suggest that Daniel bore some responsibility for understanding how his act would hurt people. She listened to me trash Hickman, then shrugged. "Well, we don't know what he was going through. It's always complicated," she said. She was right. Yet her calm assessment struck me as a telling contrast to my own emotional upset. It eventually became clear to me that my reaction was spurred by something that had more to do with me, and my identification with Pia Southam as a suicide survivor, than it did with any necessity to judge the character of the deceased Hickman. I saw in an instant that in my unusual degree of anger, I was revealing my deepest fear: that I would have another relationship, and that suicide would happen again. Here was proof that it could. In fact, statistics suggest that it is not that unusual. I could not imagine how someone could survive such tragedy a second time. It was this that had gotten under my skin, that had caused me lash out at a complete stranger, and a dead one at that. Suicide will do that to you. Maybe others could look casually at suicides as they gained passing attention in a parade of news, and not ever question the emotional basis of their judgments; for me, it seemed, there was no choice. And maybe that is not such a bad thing.

The storm has ended, a residue of wind shushing through the trees and bushes around the house. Through the screen door, I can feel a slight soft breeze, smell the soaked earth, hear drops of water falling at intervals from the eaves and splashing on the wooden backyard deck. After my own raging, I too am calm. I have picked up all the papers strewn across the floor and placed them once more in a sedate pile on the table. Enough of this trying stuff for one night, anyway. I think I was beginning to see that I could be angry at Daniel, as well as compassionate and forgiving, that one kind of emotion did not cancel out another but could coexist with it. I rise from my chair and something strange happens. I am wearing the lapis necklace Daniel gave me. Maybe I have been unconsciously pulling at it, I don't know, but as I stand up, the thin, beaded thread holding the pendant snaps at the back of my neck, slithering down the front of my tank top. I yelp with surprise and grab at the broken thread as tiny blue beads ping and dance wildly over the hardwood floor. The pendant itself tumbles from the end of the thread, spins into a corner with a clatter. I crouch on the floor, clutching the stone in one hand, trying to gather up all the beads, scanning for strays, picking out a few from where they have embedded themselves in my knees. Finally, I seem to have them all. Carefully cupping the beads, pendant, and thread, I walk to the kitchen, tear off a piece of paper towel, and place it on the counter. I gently pile everything on it and fold it into a secure envelope. I take this upstairs and put it in the jewellery case on my dresser. *I will repair it later*, I think to myself.

But I never did. Somehow, this precious gift, beautiful but broken, sits well with me as it is, more "right" than imagining myself carefully trying to restore it. Some things are beyond repair. The remains of the necklace are tucked away still.

Has someone, somehow, let go of someone else? I don't know. In the calm after the storm, I only know something feels different, maybe even better, now that I have roared at Daniel's ghost.

AT PLAY IN THE FIELDS OF 'THE SAVAGE GOD'

APRIL 1996. SITTING IN A MOVIE THEATRE at the Carlton Cinema in Toronto, watching director Bruce McDonald's darkly comic rock 'n' road film *Hard Core Logo*. The mock documentary traces the archetypal rise and fall of a punk band, complete with clashing egos, artistic dissonance, chaotic if-it's-Tuesday-it-must-be-Saskatoon life style, sleazy music-business double-crosses, and drug and alcohol abuse. It's scuzzy territory, similar to what Daniel explored in his novel *1978*. Indeed, we are told in the film that the fictional band Hard Core Logo, originally the creation of Vancouver author Michael Turner, whose novel bears the same name, launched itself that year. Depending on how you view it, it was punk's zenith, or nadir.

The film seems like the mother of all Daniel sightings to me. The band's Mohawk-hairstyled, ear-pierced lead singer, Joe Dick—played by Hugh Dillon, real-life lead singer of The Headstones—bears an extraordinary resemblance to Daniel, or so it seemed to me at the time. It's partly projection on my part; with a full head of hair, Dillon's likeness would probably fade. As with beards, there is something levelling about even semi-baldness in men, a standard-issue masculine quality that emerges when the pate is exposed just as when the lip and jawline are covered. It seems to me virtually all fair-skinned bald men could pass for Mr. Clean at a glance. The first time I saw a picture of the bearded Unabomber, I thought of several hundred slightly unconventional teachers and folk singers I have encountered over the years, not to mention Charles Manson and assorted scruffy delusionals and psychotics. It's some kind of universal male template, give or take a few variations in eye colour and facial structure.

In this case, it isn't just the exposed scalp, but also the character's demeanor, even in some uncanny way the inner life the actor intimates that reminds me so much of a certain side of Daniel: the edgy, revved-up intelligence, the fraught energy reined in by some powerful, unexpressed fear that someone might get hurt—we know not whom—the self-contempt masquerading as irreverence and cynicism, the ambivalence about success, and ultimately, the huge emotional vulnerability. It's disconcerting, yet mesmerizing, as this spectre moves in one slow-motion scene across the screen, sunglasses obliterating harrowingly sensitive eyes, mouth curled in the quintessential rebel's sneer, the gait a languorous, loose-limbed swagger.

By the end of the film, I've acclimatized somewhat to the look-alike effect and have become absorbed in the plot. Then, in the film's final scene, the camera tracks a jumpy, plastered Joe Dick out to the sidewalk in front of the hall where he and the band have just performed, apparently for the last time, having ended the show with a violent onstage explosion of hostilities that have festered for years between Dick and his best-buddy guitarist Billy Tallent. The latter has announced he is jumping ship (a ship that is sinking anyway, if only Dick would grow up and admit it) to pursue fame and fortune with a high-profile American band. In the middle of being interviewed, Dick pulls a handgun from the pocket of his coat, shoots himself in the head, and falls, blood pouring onto the sidewalk, to the gasps, groans, and "oh my Gods" of the film's faux documentarians and members of the live audience.

The whole thing leaves me spooked. My friend Karen and I

walk silently out of the theatre. "That guy really looked like Daniel," I finally say. "Yeah," Karen replies in a solemn, I-wish-it-wasn't-true tone, "I know." Obviously, the suicide packed a mean punch that I, and most of the audience, had not anticipated—though foreshadowing details are in fact littered throughout the film, as I discovered when, out of curiosity, I rented the video recently. Unlike life, you can view a movie again, fast-forwarding and rewinding to your heart's content, seeing what you may have missed, confirming or discarding your suspicions.

Dick makes at least two references to Kurt Cobain in the course of the film. One song on the soundtrack is called "Suicide Club," another, "Something Is Gonna Die Tonight." During an over-the-top group acid trip at the secluded country house of a burnt-out punk icon named Bucky Haight, there's a half-second flash of Dick putting a gun to his head, and during the final performance, he makes the gesture again. Hard to imagine that the final outcome of all of this would be such a surprise, but suicide can really be like that. Besides, the world of punk—and a good portion of modern and postmodern art, music, and literature aimed at and emanating from people under thirty—are utterly ruled by the poses and attitudes of despair. It's part of the general cultural blur, the barely noticed psychological wallpaper that adorns youthful waking lives en masse. That it might be more than a pose in some cases is cause for denial.

Yet it is unrealistic to imagine that out of all that stylized anger and aggression, there would not be casualties, and there are. We may want to hope that everyone can leave their fuck-the-world attitudes behind at the bar or concert venue and go off to happy, harmonious lives, wholesome hobbies, unperturbed relationships, purposeful work. We don't particularly want to face the fact that many come to these gatherings to let off steam precisely because they do not lead such lives. Young people are naturally drawn to music that channels the tempestuous emotions they feel, or conversely, jump-starts them out of their protective numbness, and ideally transcends it. But in much of punk, and other newer incarnations of alternative music, it can amount to just revelling in those potentially dangerous emotions.

In any form of popular expression, there's a fine line between art that springs legitimately from genuine experience and mercenary exploitation of a theme already well mined. With alternative music, there are the original artists who rage and lash out at the status quo because they understand instinctively its corrupting, or merely compromising dynamics, and are smart and sensitive enough to at least try to reject them. Then there are the imitators who swoop in and pump out their commercially driven facsimiles, maybe so far removed from an authentic sense of themselves that they hardly perceive their own fraudulence. In today's popular music business, some would say there is no line left, that the entire enterprise is driven exclusively by the goals of profit and mass popularity, and that any band that truly stood by its rebellious stance toward mainstream cultural dissemination would never "sell out" to a major record label in the first place. This attitude may be a little too pure by half; it's not necessarily evil to want lots of people to hear your music. I don't believe that Kurt Cobain, to cite the most obvious example, started out consciously manufacturing his pain, though he certainly ended up in heroin-and-celebrity-generated hell. Whether the despair is real or imagined, it's messy stuff. If I were an aspiring rock musician, I would think twice before noodling around with suicidal themes just because it's cool.

Yet the impulse to play with despair, to nurture and revere the depressive stance, is so powerful today. Since Daniel's death, I find this attitude everywhere. "Hey, Jones, dead poet! *Cool*," exclaimed the plumpish, very young man as he picked up a copy of *This Magazine*, the one containing Lynn Crosbie's article about Daniel ("Last Words," January 1996), at a booth where I was volunteering to sell magazines at the Word on the Street book festival. I looked at him as he eagerly flipped the pages. I wanted to take his puppy-fat, peach-fuzz-goateed chin firmly in my hand, turn his face toward me, and say, "*No*, honey child, dead poet *not* cool. Not cool *at all*. Daniel Jones, live poet way more cool! And don't ever forget it! Don't *ever* think suicide is cool, don't *ever* imagine you need to be depressed, drunk, or doped up to write well. DON'T!" But the young man toddled off into the milling Queen Street crowd hand-in-hand with his girlfriend before I had a chance to make any grand, crotchety statement.

Where did this notion that self-destruction is cool originate? It goes a long way back: The contemporary incarnation, from the "heroin chic" of high-fashion photo spreads to the proliferation of rock bands that glory in depression and suicide, has its roots in the Romantic era. Goethe's *The Sorrows of Young Werther* sparked a notorious spate of suicides among the poetically disposed youth of Europe in the early nineteenth century; the widely observed phenomenon of similar "contagion"-style suicides in the generations since has thus been labelled "the Werther effect."

With the end of official Romanticism in the early twentieth century, argues Alfred Alvarez in *The Savage God*, "suicide did not disappear from the arts; instead it became a part of their fabric. . . . because it threw a sharp, narrow, intensely dramatic light on life at its extreme moments, suicide became the preoccupation of certain kinds of post-Romantic writers, like Dostoevsky, who were the forerunners of twentieth-century art." Fast forward to the post-, or semi-, or techno-literate end of the century, and find that despair-fuelled rock musicians and other assorted film or TV celebrities have supplanted writers as the Werthers of our age. Their deaths by suicide or other forms of violence can spark mass response. After the suicide of Kurt Cobain in 1994, public mourning among young people reached fever pitch, and a handful of youth suicides was documented throughout North America. However, it is interesting to note that the youth suicide rate in the Seattle area where he lived and died never skyrocketed as feared. Experts who studied the statistics have since speculated that the large-scale mobilization of crisis teams in high schools, and suicide-prevention measures such as distress phone lines exclusively for young people, may actually have had the intended preventative effect.

In Japan, the 1998 suicide of popular rock singer Hideto "Hide" Matsumoto caused public paroxysms of teen grief. Fearful parents accompanied their sons and daughters to mass public services held at a Buddhist temple, where one girl did attempt suicide. Several others had already been successful. At least one teenager employed the same method of hanging with a towel that Matsumoto had used. It was a chilling replay of the spate of suicides in that country that followed the 1992 death of singer Yutaka Ozaki.

In North America, Kurt Cobain's suicide may not have led to the contagion effect parents and public health officials feared, but I've interviewed two sets of Canadian parents whose teenage sons killed themselves with a clear nod to Cobain, both in method used and as inspiration. It's hard to argue that rock music is innocuous when an anguished parent shows you a dead son's diary in which Nirvana song lyrics are prominently and frequently quoted. Another told me that the scene he found in his son's bedroom after his suicide seemed eerily set up to mimic the rock star's by-then-famous death by shotgun blast to the head.

Having said this, I don't believe censorsing or regulating rock music will solve the problem of teen suicide. That would, I'm afraid, only be shooting the messenger. Parental clucking likely drives already troubled teenagers further into their rebellious obsessions—if it bugs Mom and Dad, so much the better. The vast majority of teenagers do not, after all, kill themselves with a steady diet of this stuff, though like junk food, it might not be entirely good for them. With all suicides, you have to look at what else was going on in a person's life, sometimes deep beneath the ordinarily exposed surface, rather than blaming any one thing, including depressing or violent song lyrics.

Still, the performers themselves are often all too conscious of their dark personas, savouring and courting the dangerous side of life, vividly playing out the fantasies of their youthful fans, most of whom are at a stage in their lives when they are prone to wild projection and identification with "mentors." Jim Morrison of The Doors is the archetypal example of the brooding rock prince, whose doom-laden songs and intensely erotic sensibility endure in their power to seduce young people seeking music that reflects and amplifies their angst. Yet the early artistry of his songs eventually gave way to turgid wallowing as alcoholism changed him from an original creative talent into a fat, obnoxious drunk, masturbating on stage, wastefully dead at age twenty-seven. Morrison's grave in a Paris cemetery remains a busy centre of pilgrimage traffic from a steady stream of youthful idolators—so much so that the grave-yard's managers want to put a stop to the disruption by having Morrison's body moved elsewhere.

Deborah Curtis, wife of Ian Curtis, the depressive young lead singer of the Manchester rock band Joy Division who killed himself in 1980, observes grimly in her 1995 biography, *Touching From a Distance:* "All he needed was the excuse to follow his idols into immortality and being part of Joy Division gave him the tools to build the heart-rending reasons." On the day of his death, his wife says she awoke to the sound of—what else?—The Doors' anthem to suicidal climax, "The End," echoing loudly in her head.

At twenty-three, the obsessive and self-absorbed Curtis had a fast-growing following and mystique, sparked by a powerful stage presence and a voice hailed by U2's lead singer Bono as "holy." He was also an epileptic whose occasional violent, spas-modic fits in performance were taken by enthusiastic audiences as part of the act, though according to his wife, they were not calculated, and left Curtis himself feeling humiliated, exhausted, and physically and emotionally battered. He hanged himself only days before a scheduled first tour of North America. His wife speculates that he feared the stress of impending global fame and success. She also learned after his death that epileptics have a suicide rate five times higher than that of the average population.

Just weeks before his suicide in November 1997, INXS lead
singer Michael Hutchence participated in the filming of the movie
Limp. In it, he played a character who counsels a young rock musician to kill himself in order to secure his place in rock history. His
character refers admiringly to Cobain's death: "It was brilliant on
his part. Otherwise, he would have just been another flavour of the
day." It's unclear whether Hutchence himself believed that his own
suicide would elevate him forever to an immortality that might
elude him if he instead died quietly in his bed of a common disease
at the age of eighty-six. But the film's character does express a
sentiment that seems somehow hard-wired into rock 'n' roll.

For his part, Hutchence would appear to have been suffering a
classic case of depression at the time of his suicide. The media speculated immediately after his death by hanging in an Australian hotel
room that he had been playing some kind of kinky sex game. This
despite the fact that the singer was in many ways a textbook case of
high suicide risk: a depressed white male in his thirties taking Prozac
and recovering from drug addiction, who had expressed suicidal
feelings to friends in the weeks before, was isolated from his family
at the time, and in the middle of an ugly separation and custody
battle with his girlfriend's ex-husband, former feed-the-world guru,
Bob Geldof. Yeah, let's go with the sex-game theory.

Women have also died on the altar of beautiful rock 'n' roll
doom, via the familiar route of suicide or more ambiguous drug
overdoses, carrying on a disturbing legacy of what it means to be a
female artist. Kristen Pfaff, a guitarist with Courtney Love's band,
Hole, is one of the latest heroin heroines now resting in peace. The
centuries-old persona of the depressive, anorexic artist/poetess,
sacrificing happiness and convention for the lonely pursuit of her
gloomy art, reached full flowering in our own century, argues
Germaine Greer persuasively. In her 1995 study of the dark side of
female poetry-making, *Slip-Shod Sibyls*, she suggests that "the
versifying of agony and rage" that characterizes the work of many
female poets has limitations, both artistically and spiritually, yet

has been misguidedly celebrated and encouraged. Women such as Marina Tsvetaeva, Sylvia Plath, and Anne Sexton, all of whom eventually killed themselves, were gifted poets who gained fame and praise primarily through confessional writing out of their depressions, in the thrall of a distorted ideology that led them to spend their creative lives fuelling their own pathologies. With these poets held up as role models for generations of young women, their legacies nurture the notion that to be poetic, you must suffer, that a poem is of no real worth unless it comes soaked in the blood of your own wounds, preferably self-inflicted.

All this, Greer writes, was encouraged well into the twentieth century by a mostly male literary establishment that fostered a demeaning feminine aesthetic, a "rhetoric of petulance" that "locks women into their victim status." Citing a 1921 anthology of women's verse that included more poems by the late Amy Levy than by anyone else, Greer observes, "there can be no doubt in such a case that Levy's suicide at twenty-eight added glamour and gravitas to her reputation, for hers is not by any criterion the most impressive verse written by this group of women." Greer notes with passion that "no text, however incandescent, is worth a single human life."

Killing yourself was at one time cool on slightly different grounds than securing rock 'n' roll legend status or greater space in poetry anthologies. The roots of suicidality in art and life go deep, and are in fact as old and as universal as humanity itself. Alvarez explains how the early Christian church established suicide, or "self-murder," as a sin and, along with the state, nurtured the taboo surrounding it. The concept of immortality is a powerful one; the early church fathers were trying to discourage the alarming numbers of people who were killing themselves in hopes of becoming saints and martyrs to the glory of Christ—though perhaps, one wonders, also to escape a life of various torments, including the backbreaking labour of building cathedrals or bringing in the sheaves ad infinitum. Thus, the successful suicide became a felon, and his or her relatives were cruelly penalized.

From the zealots of Masada to the kamikaze pilots of Japan; from today's Arab suicide bombers to Jonestown's spiked–Kool-Aid drinkers and the Heaven's Gate cult members following the Hale Bopp comet to a better life aboard a spaceship—the inspirations and rationales may change, but the paradoxical human impulse to immortalize oneself through an early and exalted death has probably always been with us. The history of human culture is littered with ample evidence of a collective self-destructive instinct, a drive that impels us to enact our own deaths for various glorified reasons, or at least, to fantasize about doing so. As a species, we also groom certain individuals for self-sacrifice to quell the group's disturbing urges. Anyone writing about human psychology from Freud and Jung on has explored one or another aspect of this disturbing truth.

The connection between such aggressive urges and suicidality, from ancient times to the present, cannot be overlooked. Many well-preserved, millenia-old bodies exhumed from boggy graves throughout Europe appear to have met their deaths in some kind of ritual sacrifice. Some are young, strong specimens of humanity, wearing the garb of royalty or at least nobility, and surrounded by valuable, symbolic objects; they bear no marks of having struggled in their final moments. They have lain peacefully for centuries, on grounds that appear to have borne sacred significance for the tribal groups to which they belonged. In their resplendent clothing and jewellery, they keep the secrets of their lives and deaths, but scientists speculate that at least some of these people died their apparently ritualized deaths willingly. Perhaps if they lived today, they'd pursue careers as poets or rock musicians.

It is a powerful force, this curious and largely unconscious desire to live and die nobly and famously, and to be remembered into eternity, one that may well be the collective emotional backdrop against which many an individual suicidal drama or fantasy is played out. In our age, the psychological mechanisms at work in these fantasies may also have to do with imagining how one will look to the living—heroic, forever young—*après* one's own self-styled entry into rigor mortis, rather than with any belief in a halcyon afterlife.

In this, concepts of young death and public mourning are linked in a fascinating way. And it doesn't apply only to suicides. How else to explain the orgasmic global grief after the accidental death of Princess Diana? Extraordinarily, it was reported that the numbers of people seeking psychological counselling in Britain dropped dramatically—a whopping 50 percent—in the months after her death. Pundits theorized that the shocking event triggered a deep-seated need to grieve, that people were perhaps grieving other losses as they grieved for Diana, her death triggering their own long-overdue catharses, especially in England itself, well known for its stiff upper lips.

In a culture of celebrity worship-cum-narcissistic projection, there could be no more perfect martyr than the sometimes-suicidal Diana, no more perfect life from which to fashion a compellingly timeless, entirely modern, myth. Her death exposed how closely millions of people connected themselves to the rising and falling fortunes of the lovely princess with a heart of gold, a doomed love life, and a fabulous wardrobe. People who grumbled about the comparative lack of visceral mass grief expressed after the death of Mother Teresa missed the point. Fantasies are not politically correct; few harbour a secret longing to be, or sleep with, an aged nun, however towering her achievements and virtues. With Diana's death personally felt by a planetful of strangers, the requisite conspiracy-theory echo effect will reverberate for years to come, a standard coda to these kinds of dramas, similar to the rumours and suspicions now surrounding Kurt Cobain's death. The People's Princess joined the pantheon of modern-day human sacrifices; in this sense, she, and we in our bloodlust for beautiful losers, are perhaps more connected to those mysterious, yet beauteously preserved bog people than we might care to admit.

And so the famous, in their untimely deaths, provide some

unconscious gratification to us. Even as the unfamous fans vicariously grieve, they plug into a kind of electrical surge of feeling that makes them feel more alive, at one somehow with large and powerful forces beyond anyone's control. Perhaps the Jim Morrisons, Ian Curtises, Kurt Cobains, and Michael Hutchences of the world hook themselves and their personal confusions, their depressions, and addictions, to this same charge, creating a gateway through which to usher in their own suicides. The individual circumstances of each death may be unique, bearing all the hallmarks of contemporary culture—guns, street drugs, antidepressants, familial chaos, dissolute celebrity lifestyles—but the impulse comes from a primal place in the human psyche.

I can't say to what degree these kinds of unconscious motives operated in Daniel's case. He was familiar with the culture of suicide, read about it as extensively as he did other subjects, might even be said to have possessed an aesthete's refined appreciation of it and the nihilistic, existentialist ideas that have somehow justified it in this century. I maintain my view that these "philosophies" and "principles" are no useful guides to a depressed individual, that they merely mask underlying savage, self-destructive impulses that cannot be successfully explained or rationalized intellectually. This of course hasn't stopped a great many writers from attempting to do so, in the wake of wars, holocausts, pogroms, and other social cataclysms that traumatize, depress, and have historically given rise to such ideas.

Is it really any wonder then, that when it comes to suicide, we like to watch? *Hard Core Logo* wasn't the first or the last depiction of suicide in films, TV, theatre, books, and elsewhere to catch me off guard. Only a few weeks after Daniel's death, a well-meaning friend invited me to see a play with her, obviously hoping to take my mind off my troubles for a few hours. Not long into the performance we realized that suicide was a major subplot. I think it upset my friend more than it did me. "Are you okay?" she whispered, holding my arm as though she would lift me from my seat and briskly escort me out of the theatre if I answered no. It was almost funny. I assured her that I was fine. I think I was still too numb to care what the play had to say about anything, let alone suicide.

Later, in April, visiting my sister in London, England, she set me up one evening with a plate of comfort food in front of the TV, to watch an episode of the BBC police drama *Inside the Line.* Midway through the episode, a young policewoman leaps to her death from a Thames River tour boat; I laughed to see my sister practically lunge across the living room for the off button. In the 1990s, there's clearly little point trying to protect a mourner from reminders of suicide and its awful prevalence.

References to suicide have become pervasive, casual, even required. They weren't always so blatant or graphic. One of the earliest and most famous films featuring suicide was the sentimental *It's A Wonderful Life* (1946), where the suicide in question does not actually take place in the end, life is soundly affirmed, and everyone lives happily ever after, sure in the knowledge that in a pinch, some guardian angel will surely come to your rescue. In the early 1960s, a more sophisticated take on the subject can be found in *The Children's Hour,* featuring not just the taboo of suicide, but also lesbianism, though it's all so tastefully and understatedly handled, and the climactic glimpse of Shirley MacLaine's hanging body so shadowy, that you could almost miss what is actually going on. Perhaps some filmgoers at the time preferred to remain confused. In the early seventies, Woody Allen did a humorous turn on the subject in *Play it Again, Sam,* in which he tries to pick up a morose young woman at an art gallery by engaging her in conversation about the painting they are looking at. She gives him a flat-voiced and depressing interpretive monologue, after which he asks what she's doing that evening. "Committing suicide," she replies lugubriously, as she slinks away.

In the late 1970s, critics praised the sober maturity of the suicidal theme at the heart of *Ordinary People.* There have been numerous films since that deal with the subject with varying degrees of directness; Todd Solondz's darkly satiric film, *Happiness,* is the first

I've seen to feature a *Final Exit*-style suicide. But in most such films of the 1990s, you can forget happy endings, subtle or ambiguous shadings, or a purely light touch. I had to wonder at how far we have come in our entertainment demands while watching the 1997 film *The Devil's Advocate*, in which Keanu Reaves, to avoid losing his soul to Satan, blows out his brains with a gun, in a giant close-up. The film is as mainstream as they come, meaning that thousands upon thousands of people were watching, as I was, this almost pornographic, slow-motion display of blood and brains spraying out from the screen-size head of Reeves as the suicide-in-progress. The scene came on the heels of one almost as graphic, in which the wife of the character played by Reeves breaks the glass on the door of her mental-ward room—Al Pacino, a.k.a. Satan, has placed her in an impossible bind too—and violently gouges her wrists, with successful results on the death front.

The more recent thriller *Snake Eyes* also culminates in a cinematic shotgun blast to the head for actor Gary Sinise; *Character*, the Dutch production that won an Oscar for Best Foreign Film of 1997, follows the life and times of a diabolical bailiff who takes self-loathing to operatic extremes, courting destruction at every turn, until finally he stands in dramatic close-up at the precipice of an old warehouse shaft, plunges a knife deep into his belly, and free-falls into oblivion.

No, these days it's not a wonderful life. Have we become so psychologically numbed that we must witness such jumped-up brutality to feel we've gotten our money's worth? Why ask such a naive question? Yet as a suicide survivor, you start noticing when you find yourself culturally surrounded by suicide, particularly in the early stages of grieving, when any such passing reference seems like a jolt. Survivors report having unwelcome feelings triggered even by innocent visits to the grocery store, where they have been confronted with shelves of various grades of "suicidal" hot sauce.

The problem of navigating the outside world in the middle of your grief, without stepping on any landmines that could rip uninvited into your private emotional life, is more pressing and real than it has ever been, precisely because of the inescapability of these dime-a-dozen references. For better or worse, individuals in contemporary society have a relationship with the mass media; we bond and respond according to our own personality and prevailing mood. This multiple-personality Media can be a breezy, entertaining buddy, a concerned and thorough teacher bent on enlightening and informing, a shameless manipulator, a brainless twit, an overbearing nuisance, and worse, an insensitive, torturing bully.

Grief counsellors are often called upon to calm rattled survivors' fears that starting with the deaths of their own loved ones, suicide has become a strange and sweeping epidemic. While annual suicide figures throughout the world show a steady rise since the 1950s, that is partly accounted for by the fact that these deaths are more openly recorded now. It's also true that since the seventies, the overall yearly increases in suicides have not been significant in North America. Several years in this decade show numbers that are actually lower than some years of the 1970s. In 1994, the year Kurt Cobain died, there were 243 suicides in metropolitan Toronto, fewer than the 271 of the previous year, and the 250 of the following one. Contrary to media hype, there was no teen epidemic in Toronto, any more than there was in Seattle—only four of the 243 total were people under the age of nineteen. While statistics tend to vary within age groups and regionally, the overall rates are remarkably steady.

Based on my own experience, I'm tempted to counsel anyone who is going through the early stages of such grief to avoid films, newspapers, and TV altogether. I was stunned to find my own private mourning suddenly overlaid by mass public shock at the violent, self-inflicted death of Kurt Cobain. I winced and looked away from large close-ups of his haunted face staring from the covers of magazines everywhere. I could barely listen to news clips of Courtney Love's raw, excoriating public reading of his suicide note; I'd already read one too many, and didn't think I had anything more to learn, or any more I could take, of the genre. (Now, I hear it is possible to buy T-shirts with Cobain's suicide note printed on them.)

In the ensuing weeks, laments for the rock star and sober media analysis on the subject of suicide burgeoned. Cobain's howl-of-angst music, played obsessively on radio and TV, took on a new, more chilling spin. I tried to read some of the articles, but found little to enlighten me about this thing called suicide that now ruled my own life. Did we really need yet another trotting out of the usual facts about depression rates and Prozac? Why such overreporting about high-profile cases such as those of Cobain and White House aide Vince Foster, yet virtually none about the thousands of other people who attempt or complete suicide in any given year? While teen suicide is shocking, the media obsession with it tends to obscure the fact that most suicides are still committed by much older adults. Where are their stories? Where is any reflection of the survivor's experience? The prevention movement? An in-depth look at *why* men kill themselves with such comparative frequency? Analysis, rather than just-the-facts-Ma'am reporting, of the disturbing trend in domestic murder-suicides? Some serious questions about the prevalence of guns in American culture? Not anywhere I looked, in those early sensationalized flare-ups of herd reporting that immediately followed Cobain's death, and just as abruptly dropped from notice when the event was, a few weeks later, yesterday's news.

Turn on the TV, and find a commercial for an allergy medication in which allergens attend a psychotherapy support group and tearfully confess they want to kill themselves now that effective symptom relief for allergy sufferers has removed their purpose in life. In another prime-time commercial aired in 1998, a man threatened to jump from a high building because his breakfasts were unbearably boring; police officers talked him down with promises of a new kind of waffle. Though suicidal hot sauce may be an acceptable and standard product on grocery-store shelves, we do not similarly have among our consumer options heart-attack ice cream, or cancer smoked meat. We'd probably find that tasteless, yet we don't hesitate to trivialize suicide. Although no longer an entirely taboo subject, we fear it enough to reflexively want to make it and the despair that drives people to it somehow nonsensical.

Members of one on-line support group for suicide survivors that I joined for a time spent a good deal of their time sharing these kinds of experiences, and advising others of films and television programs to watch or avoid. It was a passionate, urgent exercise in protective networking that would not have been possible, or perhaps even necessary, on this global scale as recently as ten years ago. One man announced that he was writing a letter of protest to late-night talk show host Jay Leno, after the comedian made what the man thought was a tasteless joke about suicide. A woman counselled others who might be sensitive to avoid the film *The Game*, which contains a scene in which a man jumps to his death from the window of his mansion; the scene re-appears as a leitmotif throughout the film.

Of course, sometimes these surprise appearances of suicide come with genuine intelligence and wit. The surreal French film *Delicatessen* (1991) contains a shockingly funny subplot featuring a beleaguered and hysterical woman who fails to do herself in, foiled repeatedly as she tries ever more ludicrously elaborate means. The humour may be bleak, yet the irreverence here says something too true about the human condition—and in a highly stylized film about cannibalism, the suicidal antics seem downright tame.

The plot of one episode of CBC's internationally acclaimed satirical program, *The Newsroom*, revolved around the threat of a failed screenwriter to kill himself on camera. The news programmers are of course beside themselves with glee, and so intent on getting the great clip that they are visibly distressed when the man begins to reconsider his plan. With thoughts ever on the ratings, scumball news director George sets assiduously to the task of rekindling the man's despair. A similar sly comment even appears in the movie *Spice World*. When the Spice Girls' pompous-ass manager pulls out a noose and threatens to hang himself after the group refuses to perform a scheduled concert, the dim-witted documentarian who stumbles after them throughout the film noses in with his camera. When the manager recants his threat, the man is openly morose. "There goes the best thing in the film," is his nakedly mercenary comment on the matter. Even kids, and the parents who accompanied them to a fluffy summer film, were getting their dose of suicide-inspired cynicism.

It's not that exploring suicide, even facetiously, is inherently wrong or dangerous. Studies on the links between fictional, filmed, or televised treatments of suicide and its actual incidence have yielded contradictory results. Suicide experts have found some relationship between teenage suicide and televised portrayals, but some are inclined to hedge, and to downplay the possibility that the Werther effect might successfully transmit itself through mass media. "To the extent that fictional presentations of suicide may serve as stimuli for imitative behavior, the effect appears to depend on a complex interaction among characteristics of the stimulus, the observer of that stimulus, and conditions of time and geography." This is the cautious conclusion of Alan L. Berman, an American psychologist and leading suicide expert. I believe he means that someone would have to be leaning strongly toward suicide anyway to be triggered into action by something like a TV program. It may be that film makers and television programmers don't necessarily have to worry about being held responsible for real suicides, should they focus on the subject in fictional form. Still, its use in plots does seem gratuitous at times, as though to have your film, novel, or television program taken seriously, at one with the Zeitgeist of the moment, you had better throw in a suicide.

Some artists do seriously explore or touch on the subject. Our death instincts, in the form of self-destructive impulses, are real, and often denied in our day-to-day lives, sometimes astonishingly so, given how prevalent random violence has become. So why not explore these impulses and the circumstances that surround them, this dangerous real terrain? Several recent films, including *The*

Hanging Garden, Girls' Town, Once Were Warriors, and even the popular comedy *The Full Monty,* don't insult the humanity of either their characters or the audience. For actors, this trend perhaps means that just as they must decide whether or not to do nude scenes, they'll also now have to decide whether to add suicide scenes to their repertoires. Many have already done so—as well as the gunshots to the head of Hugh Dillon in *Hard Core Logo,* Gary Sinise in *Snake Eyes,* and Keanu Reeves in *The Devil's Advocate,* suicides have recently been portrayed on film by Kathy Bates (*Primary Colors*), Vanessa Redgrave (*Deep Impact*), William H. Macy (*Boogie Nights*), and Courtney Love (*The People vs. Larry Flynt*), to name just a few. I did wonder particularly how the widow Love felt as she played the character of a junkie dying of AIDS who drowns herself in a large bathtub.

I've noted my own feelings and reactions too, for as with *Hard Core Logo,* I found as I watched other films that I rarely saw it coming, and yet couldn't believe that was the case, once it had happened. My emotional response varied greatly. In a thriller like *The Game,* you don't exactly bond with the characters, and so when a minor one plunges to his death, it's hardly heartbreaking—unless, of course, as was pointed out at the suicide survivor on-line support group, you've recently lost a loved one in a similar manner. But then I watched the film *Carrington,* based on the real life story of Dora Carrington, a Bloomsbury denizen who had a long and curiously intense relationship with the homosexual Lytton Strachey. I felt as though the wind had been kicked out of me when the scene came in which the painter Carrington, played by Emma Thompson, calmly prepares to shoot herself. My heart sank as she briskly gathered up her brushes, paints, and palette and threw them into a garbage can in her studio, moments before she matter-of-factly positions the long-barrelled gun against her chest and, still standing, pulls the trigger.

Something about this image of the artist simply giving up, saying, "To hell with it, I can't do it anymore," resonated in a terrible way for me. How difficult it seems for so many of the gifted to find the conditions in which they can make their art without destroying themselves. How many great creations in images, music, and words have been lost to the world through suicide? Naturally, I was thinking of Daniel, and all of his lost words.

More than anything, beyond the particular, personal ways I have come to view Daniel's suicide, I have been perplexed as I contemplated all the stories about suicide, in a riot of forms, that have sped past me on the hectic currents of popular culture over the past five years. Why is it, I have wanted to know, that while we seem immersed in images of suicide and attitudes of despair, we are stunned, disbelieving, at a complete loss to understand what happened when a real suicide is forced upon us? Something just didn't add up, as I regarded my own, and all of our collective, psychological responses.

TRAVELS WITH MY GRIEF

TRAUMA HAS A WAY OF TURNING PEOPLE into detectives. In particular, people traumatized by a suicide feel compelled to find out more about the subject, perhaps to alleviate feelings of guilt, perhaps for the solace of knowing they are not alone in their tragedy, or perhaps, more altruistically, to gain and pass on some understanding that might spare someone else a terrible experience.

After several years of research, I could paper the walls of my entire home with pamphlets, brochures, and handouts on suicide prevention—the world does not want for helpful information on how to spot depression, how to assess a person's risk for suicide, or how to deal with these situations should they arise. Yet I know that as I write, someone is in the midst of commiting suicide, someone who never read a pamphlet, never received therapy or medication, and may not even be able to put a name to what it is they are suffering. Someone else is finding that person dead, someone just as much in the dark, and beginning his or her own nightmare, one that probably includes self-recrimination. Soon, this new survivor will be on the waiting list of a bereavement support group, and will begin an education and healing process that he or she will wish had begun long before the tragedy took place.

I'm not talking about a small, ignorant group of lost souls. I'm talking about people I meet all the time, socialize with, have counselled as a volunteer. People who never gave a thought to depression that they later had to acknowledge affected whole generations of their family, who thought suicide was an ugly thing that happened to others, something so removed from their consciousness that they could barely believe it when it crashed in on them. People who think therapy is only for the very sick or weak. Those who hold such views have so much more to contend with when a suicide does happen, such an ingrained pattern of denial and ignorance to chip away at. Conferences such as those held annually by the Canadian Association for Suicide Prevention (CASP) or the American Association of Suicidology (AAS) attract hundreds with an interest in the subject, indeed who have devoted whole careers to it, but I find many people still look at me with astonishment and even repulsion when they hear the term "suicidology." At the AAS convention I attended in Memphis in 1997, a large banner was strung across the lobby of the Peabody Hotel, causing many guests to point, gasp, and laugh nervously among themselves.

Or perhaps in a particular case of suicide, ignorance isn't the problem: The suicidal person in question was no stranger to the mental-health system, having made previous attempts. Help had been offered, but the suicide occurred anyway. In spite of obvious forewarning, the loss will be no less acute for loved ones, the perplexity about how it might have been stopped no less keenly felt.

In the beginning, I believe my own search for answers to the paramount question of why Daniel had killed himself was based on the misapprehension that the event was somehow like a giant, brain-teasing puzzle—if ony I could find that last crucial piece and put it into place I would have a definitive answer—or at least a complete picture to hang onto, a tangible something to stand in the space where Daniel used to be. But I came to see that the whole thing was more like a disastrous airplane crash. I could comb the site for each and every scrap of the exploded wreck, painstakingly reassemble it too, until the fuselage stood, bearing all its cracks, dents, and fault lines. Still, it would never amount to what it was before the accident, and the all-important black box—Daniel himself—was and forever would be missing.

Back in January 1997, as I embarked on research for this book, I didn't intend to explore the stories of three kids who had killed themselves in Calgary jails. I came to the city to visit the Suicide Information and Education Centre, to find answers to nagging personal questions, and to questions about the nature and effectiveness of current approaches to suicide prevention. But when I left the airport and crawled into a cab, a copy of the *Calgary Herald* sat waiting for me on the back seat. SUICIDE IN ALBERTA screamed the banner head above a story about a teenager named Isaac Mercer, who had killed himself only the day before. This story was accompanied by another about nine other people who had killed themselves in custody over the past eighteen months. I hadn't expected such a welcome mat, and felt an awful sense of having arrived, grimly enough, in the right place at the right time. I could hardly resist saying, "Driver, take me to the suicide archive at once, and step on it, will you?" Over the weeks I spent in Alberta, I was to discover many sad and disturbing things about suicide and how it is, and tragically isn't, prevented.

Karen Payne says her first thought when she answered a knock at the door of her northwest Calgary home and saw two police officers standing there was *What else has Jesse done?* It was seven o'clock in the evening on May 16, 1996. Earlier that day, Karen had received a phone call at work from her fourteen-year-old son, who told her that he had been taken into custody, after complaints from a local mall that he and a group of other teenagers had been causing a disturbance. Jesse was charged with breaching a probation order that he attend school regularly. What Karen felt on hearing that news was relief.

After a hellish year of coping with Jesse's disturbed, and disturbing, behaviour, Karen thought her son's case would now be taken more seriously by someone among the multitude of professionals who had passed judgment on what his problems might be: "Conduct disorder" and "attention deficit disorder" were just two theories advanced. At the very least, she knew where he was, something she didn't take for granted, since Jesse had begun disappearing for weeks at a time, seemingly indifferent to the upset he caused his family, and proudly aware that as of the ripe age of thirteen, he was not required by law to reside in his parents' home. When the officers knocked at the door, Karen and her husband, Bruce, were sitting at the supper table with their three other children, then aged ten, twelve, and fifteen, discussing what they would do next to help their troubled son.

But when the officers told the Paynes that Jesse had hanged himself in a police holding cell a couple of hours earlier, and that his body now lay awaiting identification at the Bow Valley Centre morgue, the evening that had begun with a sense of hope became, says Karen, "surreal." Fifteen-year-old Matt ran from the house, shouting and crying. Karen called friends, who arrived shortly after to comfort the other two children and round up Matt, who had headed to his own friend's house. The cops, whom Bruce had told to leave, went and sat in their cruiser down the street.

At about 8:30, Bruce finally called the Bow Valley Centre. The voice at the other end told him his son was not dead, but in intensive care. The staff had been wondering why it was taking the Paynes so long to get there. With this stunning news, Bruce and Karen left for the hospital, but first called Matt's friend's house, to tell their son that his brother was still alive. The traumatized teenager, along with the family friend who'd gone looking for him, eventually made their way to the parked cruiser and asked what was going on. "Well," said one of the officers, "he's not dead yet, but he will be." Matt declined the offer of a ride to the hospital.

It was six days before the Paynes consented to the removal of the life-support system that had been keeping Jesse's body alive. He had hanged himself with his sock, in spite of the presence of surveillance monitors that were supposed to be regularly checked by staff. Between May 16 and May 22, the official date of Jesse's death, waves of distraught teenagers from the boy's neighbourhood and junior high school filled the hospital's waiting room and kept vigil on the lawns. It seemed no one believed it was happening, or knew what to do, including police officers who stood post outside Jesse's room until Karen asked them to leave the family alone. In a nearby quiet room, an officer she assumed had been sent to offer some explanation for what had happened to her son instead asked point-blank: "What are you planning to do about the press?" Karen says she didn't understand what the officer was getting at. Then an article appeared in the *Calgary Sun* with the headline COPS TRAUMATIZED BY YOUTH HANGING. Karen finally realized that if she didn't do something about the media, her family's tragedy would end up as fodder for a cruel and caricatured version of events that placed the police as hapless victims of a young hooligan whose suicide in custody could never have been prevented, and whose death, albeit untimely, wouldn't be much lamented anyway.

"It was my idea to release a picture of Jesse," she says. "I wanted people to know that he was a person, that he had a family and friends who cared about him. I wanted to counter the demonization that was happening. It was like a bad movie. I thought, *This is my child.* And people don't want to face it, but this could be anybody's kid." So, says Karen, she finally agreed to talk openly to the media about Jesse. And her husband called a lawyer.

In May 1997, I returned to Calgary to do more research. Almost one year to the day after her son's death, Karen Payne agreed to an interview, and suggested we meet at a downtown Calgary café called the Vicious Circle. Appropriate. I was getting used to hearing the complex, dumbfoundingly sad stories of suicides, their misfortunes painstakingly laid out for me by grieving loved ones left to circle the past again and again, regarding it obsessively through filters of guilt, anger, regret, and blame that radiate from a fixed point of sorrow.

Unfortunately, Karen wasn't the only parent in Calgary at the time who was grieving a son's suicide in police custody. The mandatory inquiry into Jesse's death was not yet under way when, four months later, an eighteen-year-old native youth named Kris Roulette hanged himself, using bed sheets attached to cell bars, at the Calgary Remand Centre. Plagued by drug and alcohol problems, Roulette was charged with car theft and had been moved to the regular cells from the Centre's hospital unit, where he had told a nurse and a doctor that he felt suicidal only hours before his death. Two inmates in adjoining cells listened in horror to the sounds of Roulette strangling himself. They shouted for help, but no one came until the boy was already dead.

In January 1997, only six weeks after the inquiry into Jesse Payne's death ended, seventeen-year-old Isaac Mercer was brought into Calgary police custody from the treatment facility for troubled adolescents where he lived, on suspicion of a home-invasion robbery. An hour after a worker at the home had alerted the police that Mercer was suicidal, the teenager, left alone in a holding room, hanged himself from a ceiling sprinkler fixture with the shoelaces from his sneakers.

In all three cases, many were called upon to do some explaining, including the police, jail employees, social workers, nurses, physicians, and psychologists who, although they came into contact with the boys in the hours, days, weeks, and months leading up to their deaths, somehow collectively failed to prevent them from happening. Because they were so young, because they killed themselves, and because they did it in publicly funded institutions, the three boys have posthumously garnered public attention and raised uncomfortable questions in the province's media and criminal justice system. No one much likes the answers.

Each year, hundreds of Albertans, among several thousand Canadians, take their own lives. Old people do it, kids do it, but mostly men between the ages of twenty-four and forty-five do it. Right now in Canada, Quebecers do it more than people in any other province; aboriginal men in Canada do it more than any other demographic group in the world. And it's well known that people in prison or police custody, especially young people, are at significantly higher risk for suicide than the general population. We read or hear of these things and think, *Isn't it awful.* Most of us don't really know what to say or do beyond that.

It's certainly taking a while for the Alberta justice system to figure out what to do. The report from Jesse Payne's inquiry was a scant two pages. Judge A. A. Fradsham acknowledged the tragedy, but seemed content with the way the police had handled Jesse in custody, and was satisfied that they had taken measures to prevent such an occurrence in future: They placed a metal plate over the door grill where he'd hanged himself, and said they'd keep youths in cells nearer the "general counter." The judge's sole recommendation was that if possible, juveniles should not be left alone in cells, but should be placed together with other juveniles.

Yet Fradsham's recommendation was not enough to save the life of Isaac Mercer, who was placed in a cell alone, only six weeks after the Payne inquiry wrapped up. This time, the police and many others were held to account for the tragedy. The January 1998 report from the inquiry into Isaac Mercer's death was forty-one pages long. Written by provincial youth court judge Hugh Landerkin, it delved deep into the problem, and offered scathing criticism of the police, workers at Isaac's group home, his divorced parents, and indeed, an entire society that blinds itself to the cumulative adverse conditions that lead to the suicide of a vulnerable young person. He called for an independent criminal investigation of police conduct in Isaac's case, and he got it. Although Justice Minister Jon Havelock had been unwilling to take any action after Jesse Payne's death (and was unavailable at the time for interviews), he leapt to crusade after Landerkin's report came out, suddenly more than willing to hold court before the media: "This is a pressing matter," he told reporters in grave, urgent tones. "It was a tragic chain of events." Havelock's swiftly held probe concluded that there had been no criminal wrongdoing on the part of the police, but conceded that officers had made some mistakes in their handling of the case. Now, Calgary Police Chief Christine Silverberg is going to court to challenge Judge Landerkin's report, arguing that he went beyond his mandate in his statements and recommendations, particularly in his suggestions of possible criminal liability on the part of the force. The chief has also launched a countersuit against Jesse Payne's parents, who, along with Isaac Mercer's father and Kris Roulette's mother, have launched lawsuits against those they consider responsible for their sons' untimely deaths.

Since the police have been cleared of any criminal negligence or intent, Chief Silverberg's time might be better spent acknowledging errors that have been independently observed by the two inquiries, and ensuring that her staff is more equipped with the knowledge and skills needed to deal with people at risk for suicide in custody. Under his recommendation titled "Mandatory Suicide Education," Judge Landerkin wrote:

> Here [with Isaac Mercer] was a prior suicide attempt. Here was a history of conduct disorder and social dysfunction and family breakdown. Tracking Isaac's behaviour and considering the criteria noted in the [psychiatric textbook] DSM-1V, I come to the objective conclusion that Isaac was on a suicide pathway. Lengthy police detention put him in a suicide

zone. A warning existed. Simple preventive measures could have been taken. Further investigations should have been undertaken immediately. With knowledge about suicide, the police officers here would have been more sensitive to what was going on and acted in a more positive way. If this was the case, perhaps we would not be here today . . . . Testimony before this inquiry shows that we now have the knowledge, in Calgary, to teach us how to better prepare ourselves against such potential tragedies. Why this has not been done to date escapes me. No good reason exists.

Tucked away among industrial low-rises in Calgary's southwest end, the Suicide Information and Education Centre (SIEC) operates without fanfare with a paid staff of six through both provincial and private funding of roughly $600,000 annually. But its modest appearance is misleading. SIEC has been called the best archive of literature and other materials on the subject of suicide in the world. Typically, Canadians don't know about it, exhibit any pride, or celebrate what could rightly be considered a unique and precious resource. Yet researchers from Los Angeles to Liberia regularly visit the decade-old centre's library, access its vast and rapidly growing database, or cruise its award-winning website. There they can find books, articles, bibliographies, and newsletters on anything from the link between suicide and sexual abuse to the higher-than-average suicide risk among adolescent boys in custody, and what has been done in some jurisdictions to minimize it. These research materials reflect a huge shift in attitudes toward suicide, a greater willingness—at least from some people—to explore the subject and compile a growing repository of knowledge that is the basis for suicidology.

The centre is also the coordination base for a variety of suicide-prevention training programs designed for everyone from teachers to police officers. Developed over the last decade, they are now exported worldwide to great acclaim. When the program was implemented in the early nineties by a county public-health unit in California, it won a commendation of excellence from the state's governor. And in 1997 here in Canada, it received a prestigious award from the Canadian Mental Health Association for a program designed in conjunction with RCMP detachments in several aboriginal communities throughout the country. Related programs are also offered under the auspices of Living Works, currently run by Calgary psychiatrist Bryan Tanney and two colleagues.

The programs are designed to teach simple techniques that anyone can use to identify people at high risk for suicide and deal with them appropriately. While it would be impossible to prove that such training could have prevented the suicides of the three boys in Calgary, one thing is certain: Any police officer or jail employee who took this course would learn that recently incarcerated young males are among the highest-risk groups for suicide in the entire human population, and the last thing you do with a suicidal person is leave them alone for hours on end, with something that can be turned into a means of self-destruction. But for reasons that won't be fully explained until current investigations and lawsuits surrounding the boys' deaths are resolved, the Calgary police declined to avail themselves of the centre's highly praised services, despite being offered training twice in the past five years.

In light of all of this, it is tempting to focus on police ignorance and negligence as the sole cause of these untimely deaths. But that would be simplistic, and suicide is anything but simple. In the case of each of these boys, troubled histories brought them into contact with any number of professionals who might be expected to know something about suicide. And among the most cruel ironies surrounding these deaths is the fact that the province of Alberta did for a time lead the country, and much of the world, in fostering greater awareness of suicide—even, for a decade, hiring a provincial suicidologist as a watchdog over the problem and an advocate for prevention. The position was phased out several years ago.

The "Alberta model" of suicide prevention, designed in the early eighties by an ambitious group of psychologists, psychiatrists and social workers (some of the same people who now offer Living Works), never really got off the ground, even though it is still written about glowingly. The prevention training programs, the information centre, and the now defunct suicidologist were all components of the original model, but other elements, including a state-of-the-art research facility affiliated with the University of Calgary, never saw the light of day. The idea for the centre was conceived during Alberta's oil boom, but appeals to the government for funding of a plum academic institution coincided with the oil bust, and were quickly moved to the frills category on provincial priority lists. Nothing like it existed in Canada until a Chair of Suicide Studies was established in 1997 at the University of Toronto, with a $2-million endowment from the university and from funds raised by the mother of a manic-depressive doctor who killed himself at the age of thirty-six.

But there is a final, regrettable element to all of this, one that makes it impossible to view these deaths as merely the personal tragedies of three unlucky families. The whole notion of the Alberta model was based on the fact that a 1976 provincial task force, appointed by the Alberta government in response to a suicide rate that was markedly higher than in other provinces, produced a report stating:

> . . . with few exceptions, gatekeepers [ie. police, physi-
> cians, social workers, etc.] have a low level of awareness
> that suicide and non-accidental self-injury constitute a
> significant social problem. Fewer still are aware of the
> potential in their own roles for prevention, intervention
> and postvention . . . we have a long way to go on the road
> to an effective suicide prevention program in Alberta. At

present, we are not even looking at causes; at best, we are making a half-hearted attempt at intervention in cases where suicide is already a crisis situation.

As it happened, I was able to interview the man who had chaired the task force, Menno Boldt, a professor of sociology and long-standing supporter of the Samaritans, the British originators of anonymous telephone distress-line counselling, whose only Canadian branch is based in Lethbridge. In preparation for his retirement, he donated his large personal archive of suicide literature to executive director Hilde Schlosar, who I had met at the Canadian Association for Suicide Prevention conference in Toronto a few months earlier, and who, over the course of two years, has become a friend. She thought Boldt would agree to be interviewed. Indeed, he seemed thrilled to talk, and heartened that someone was writing about what he feels is the often neglected issue of suicide.

Boldt grew up in Standoff, on the Blood reserve, the son of Mennonite schoolteachers, and so it was natural for him to follow a scholarly interest in aboriginal people. His 1991 book on treaty rights is called *Surviving as Indians*. In 1973, when Boldt was writing about aboriginal leadership, he once consulted a local elder named Leroy Little Bear. "It was one day early in the winter, and we drove by the cemetery at St. Mary's Residential School. As we were going past we could see that there were six new graves that had been dug there since the snowfall. It was such an astonishing sight. I was haunted by it. It turned out that of the six, three had committed suicide. Now this is just one small community, and I thought, 'There's something happening here that's unconscionable.'"

Boldt wrote a letter to the minister of social services and community health, expressing his concern about the high incidence of suicide in native communities. There was some mild interest, though nothing came of it right away. But others were concerned about the province's overall suicide rate, especially when the arrival of a new provincial coroner in 1974 brought a 100 percent increase in the number of suicides reported as cause of death. Times were changing, not just in Alberta, but elsewhere too; coroners who had once felt compelled to bow to families' feelings and social taboos by officially pronouncing suicide deaths "accidents" were now more inclined to state the ugly truth.

Eventually, what had begun as a single task force to look into the high incidence of both traffic fatalities and suicides was split into two, and Boldt was asked to chair the task force on suicide. For two years, he and a dozen colleagues scoured the literature on suicide, analyzed statistics, and conducted interviews. The document they produced is impressive, filled with humane intentions and practical recommendations on how to implement them. While acknowledging that the root causes of suicide are complex, the report concluded that preventing suicides, intervening when they appear to be in progress, and dealing with the consequences of those that occur are basic social responsibilities. It specifically stated the urgent need to train members of the community—teachers, doctors, nurses, social workers, the police—to identify high-risk individuals and act according to standardized protocols. It cited research from the Samaritans in England that showed downturns in the incidence of suicide in places where such procedures had been instituted.

Twenty-two years later, not much had changed. Why such difficulty marrying the impressive wealth of Alberta-based knowledge and expertise in the field of suicide prevention with the province's people and institutions who could most use it? The position of the police, stated repeatedly at the inquiry into Jesse Payne's death—that there was absolutely nothing more they could have done to prevent it—is baffling. In fact, an inordinate amount of attention was paid during the various fatality inquiries to the angle of the dangle of cameras monitoring the rooms where the boys did themselves in (suggesting that certain crannies of these spaces could not be seen through the monitors, though there were also suggestions that the monitors were not regularly checked), as though a proper grasp of geometry was more important in preventing suicides than a rudimentary understanding of psychology.

While no one would expect the police to hire jail staff with doctorates in the subject, their refusal to admit that their procedures might be improved with a bit of readily available training seemed unreasonable to some, including Jesse Payne's mother. She heard a reference to the Suicide Information and Education Centre on the radio and went down herself to see what she could learn after her son's death. She was stunned to find that an entire literature existed, much of it written by and for police officers and other professionals who work with young offenders, on the issue of suicide prevention, including case studies from New Zealand and several American states where youth suicide in custody had been brought down to zero. "If a housewife can walk in and read this stuff, why can't the police?" she wanted to know.

Karen Payne is convinced that her son was suffering from an undiagnosed mental disorder that even he had begun to acknowledge. In the last two weeks of his life, she thought they'd at last found hope, in the form of a social worker at the Woods Home for troubled adolescents. "He told her that he knew he had a problem, if only he could figure out what it was. He said he didn't want to live this way anymore." Three years later, she feels motivated to campaign for changes to the whole system of treating troubled adolescents and young offenders. "Of course I feel like I failed Jesse! I think we all failed Jesse," says Karen.

Maybe the police, like many others, are just in denial; it's not as though anyone particularly wants to think about suicide until it has blown its way uninvited into our lives. Experts cannot offer the solace of massively reduced suicide rates as an overall result of their knowledge. "Like the blind men who grab different parts of the elephant and misidentify the beast, suicide experts, exploring suicide from their own perspectives, end up supplying only part of the whole," writes American journalist George Howe Colt in his 1991 book, *The Enigma of Suicide*. He quotes Shneidman: "Suicide is a

biological, sociocultural, interpersonal, dyadic, existential malaise."
Howe Colt goes on to comment ruefully, "Shneidman's definition is
cumbersome, but it may be the most accurate we have."

What is clear is that Jesse did not get meaningful help for the
problems from which he was so evidently suffering. In a fragmented social services system of overburdened agencies, information is rarely formally passed from one jurisdiction to another. The
fact that Jesse had been deemed at risk for suicide in at least one
official file during this tumultuous period was hidden deep in
bureaucratic oblivion by the time he was left to sit alone for hours
in a police holding unit. The file also contained an angry suicide
note written a year before his death, and found in his bedroom by
his mother, who talked to Jesse about it and passed it on to a
psychologist. But not only was thirteen-year-old Jesse free under
the law to come and go as he pleased at his parents' home, he was
also free to cancel his psychological counselling sessions. At the
inquiry, the psychologist whose appointment he failed to show up
for the day before his death said that she did not consider him a
suicide risk at the time—and blamed his parents for the many
missed appointments. The Paynes have since attempted to retrieve
the suicide note, and other documents about their son, but have
been told that the note and several files have gone missing.

Commenting on how such a tragic situation could develop,
psychiatrist Bryan Tanney, who spoke as an expert witness at the
inquiry, says, "You have to look at a long chain of people in society
who let that kid down. This [suicide in custody] is just the end
result." The Paynes themselves felt sidelined throughout the
inquiry, and Karen was frustrated when the judge said he would
allow her to speak, even though, he pointed out, she wasn't an
expert. The two were outraged when Isaac Mercer died, as though
no one had learned anything from their own son's death. "Kris's
death was bad enough, but Isaac's was like a kick in the stomach.
We knew we couldn't keep quiet about it then, or nothing would
ever change," says Karen.

It was some comfort that the judge presiding over the inquiry into Kris Roulette's suicide in June 1997 was less inclined than Judge Fradsham to accept the authorities' version of events—especially when he learned that they had failed to inform him that there were witnesses, in the form of two inmates. He halted the proceedings until they could be brought in to testify. In his recommendations, he noted that the general practitioner who deemed Kris ready to go into the Remand Centre's adult population from the hospital appeared not to have much psychological expertise; he had been hired on a short-term contract, and was, as Kris Roulette's mother, Debbie, learned when she looked him up in the phone book, ordinarily a specialist in hair transplants. The judge's report therefore concluded that assessments regarding the mental fitness of inmates should be conducted only by a psychologist or psychiatrist. It also came to light that even though a nurse wrote in Kris's file that he was suicidal, jail guards were never told this, and so the judge recommended that information of this kind be routinely passed from nursing staff to custody officers. With an added note of compassion, he recommended that native elders and counsellors be made available to native inmates in crisis, since Kris had apparently pleaded to talk to someone who might understand his current problem, which, in hindsight, appears so obviously to have been suicidal feelings compounded by drug and alcohol withdrawal.

But it was the Landerkin report into Isaac Mercer's death that seemed to make its mark with the public. While the media had been inclined to portray Jesse Payne and Kris Roulette as bad asses, whose suicides might actually lift a burden from the community, Landerkin's recommendations were reported in the *Calgary Herald* with an article that looked more sympathetically at Isaac's life, with touching photos of him as a tow-headed tot cuddling a cat, and as a slightly older kid with a look of delight as he emerged from a swimming pool. It was natural to wonder whether Isaac Mercer might still be alive if a report like Judge Landerkin's had arisen from Jesse Payne's fatality inquiry; and equally, to wonder whether

Jesse Payne and Kris Roulette might too still be alive, if at many critical junctures in their young lives, the adults who were charged with dealing with them had had the benefit of the suicide-prevention expertise for which their province is world-renowned.

And yet, anyone in the field of suicide prevention will also tell you that even with the most exhaustive knowledge at hand and well-intentioned social programs in place, not every suicide can be predicted or prevented; it is, in the sociological jargon, a "multi-factoral" problem; and, it's difficult, if not impossible, to measure the cause-and-effect relationship of suicide-prevention measures to a suicide that doesn't happen (in which case, it isn't part of any statistic). That Canada's rate of suicide was the same in 1995 as it was in 1975, for instance, does not necessarily mean that all prevention measures instituted over two decades were abject failures; for all we know the rate would be much higher without them.

Probes and inquiries end, media attention shifts, police continue doing their often unenviable jobs, professionals move on to grapple with other problems in their massive caseloads, and politicians decide which stance on which issue of the moment is most likely to win public support. But the parents of Jesse, Kris, and Isaac will, for the rest of their lives, deal with the biological, sociocultural, interpersonal, existential malaise that is suicide.

Isaac's father, Ken Mercer, a member of the collection crew of the Calgary sanitation department who describes himself as "a bit of a redneck," says he was stung on numerous occasions by the attitudes of his co-workers, some of whom have more or less said that Isaac was, after all, a delinquent, and well, what do you expect? "Nobody deserves to die," he says. "Not like that. I'm aware that the police don't want to make an arrest a pleasant experience for a kid, but if you're going to push someone close to the edge, you better be prepared to haul them back by the scruff of the neck when they start to go over it."

Losing Isaac has caused Mercer to reevaluate his entire life, agonizing over various events and decisions that might have weighed heavily on his son, searching for clues as to why it happened. It's also sent him on something of a spiritual and philosophical quest, looking, he says, for the right balance between the values of discipline and justice, love and forgiveness. He has visited a Buddhist theologian at the University of Calgary, and sought counselling from a Blackfoot elder: "He said that this emptiness from the loss of my son could be filled by embracing other children. And I am trying to do that. My other two kids seem to be doing okay. And there are friends of Isaac's who come and talk to me, and I want to be there for them."

Mercer has been reading too, everything from *My Son . . . My Son* by Iris Bolton, considered a classic in suicide bereavement literature, to more general philosophical self-help books like *The Road Less Travelled* and *A Course in Miracles*. I ask Mercer if he ever thought he'd be doing any of this, and he shakes his head, cracks a smile, and laughs a bit for the first and only time during the interview. "I guess you could say I'm a Buddhist redneck now."

In the wake of her son's death, Debbie Roulette is trying to gain some control over what has been a difficult and chaotic life, looking for a new place to live outside a tough Calgary neighbourhood where she doesn't feel safe, hoping to resume some high-school upgrading. She says she was reasonably happy with the recommendations that came out of the inquiry, but still feels that native kids in particular get the bummest of bum raps when they come in contact with the law. At fourteen, she tells me, she was herself placed in a girls' detention centre, where she was sexually molested by a staff member. Two years later, she gave birth to Kris, and would eventually have two more boys whom she raised as a single mother. "Nobody teaches you to be a parent," she says, in a voice tinged with anger and sadness. She too is well aware of the easy judgments afoot as to why Kris got himself into such trouble in the first place. "I did my best. I loved Kris completely and gave him and my other sons everything I could. Kris was no angel, but he was a soft and gentle boy inside. He should never have been put in that cell."

Roulette said she wanted to go camping with her son's ashes, somewhere in the interior of B.C., but hadn't yet been able to do it. "He always wanted to go there," she says, her gaze shifting to somewhere far off behind my head. "It's just too bad it has to be after he's dead."

For a time, Debbie and Karen Payne met regularly to discuss their cases and what strategy to take in campaigning for changes in the system they feel was instrumental in their sons' deaths. It's an alliance based on shared tragedy, but Debbie says Karen is one of the best friends she's ever had. Last year, when she couldn't make ends meet, she opened her door to find several bags full of groceries from Karen. "No one has done anything like that for me in my life," says Debbie.

I hadn't intended it, but my visit to Calgary made it impossible to ignore what amounted to a perfect object lesson in the question of why, with all the knowledge at hand, so many suicides are not prevented. The best and most frank answer I have come across to date remains that of Judge Hugh Landerkin: no good reason.

SURVIVORS
AND OTHER STRANGERS

FOR NORMA BEATTIE, THE SUICIDE of her father when she was fifteen years old was an insidiously catastrophic event. More than four decades later, it still reverberates through her life. Like many of the survivors I interviewed, Norma was introduced to me by a friend. She was completing an undergraduate degree in religious studies at McMaster University in Hamilton, Ontario, her home town. She had raised a family, been divorced, and returned to school, where she was spurred by nagging questions about her own past to focus her studies on the philosophical and spiritual aspects of suicide.

"I came home from the beach, and was told my father was in the hospital, he had taken all his pills, and he died, and that was the end of that." There was no funeral, as though to mark the death would be to accord respect where it wasn't due: Jim Beattie had been a difficult man, who caused much domestic strife throughout Norma's childhood and adolescence. Her parents were separated at the time of his suicide. "The death wasn't discussed at home. I know I talked about it with my friends, but I felt like some kind of freak," she says. Her brother, six at the time, told her many years later that he hadn't really accepted until he was twenty-one that his father was dead and would never return. One older sister, twenty at the time of the suicide, took her own life at the age of fifty-one—the same age their father had been when he died.

Norma believes her father sexually abused her sister, and is haunted by memories of violence she witnessed and didn't understand at the time. "I'm a naturally cheerful person myself, but the sadness is there, it is part of my foundation," says Norma, who for years, felt a persistent sense of irresolution about her father's death. Her grief of course deepened after her sister's suicide in 1987. "With a suicide, you feel that any dialogue you might have had is truncated, but the body is still littering the ground wherever you go. It's hard to move through that body. All there is is silence. It has been silenced, or you have been silenced." Her own pain became more acute—she would scream and cry uncontrollably while driving alone in her car—and her questions about how this tragedy had come to be visited on her family became more urgent. She didn't even know what had become of her father's body. Finally, her mother told her it had been donated to the University of Toronto's school of medicine. Norma called the school, and learned that her father was buried in Toronto's Mount Pleasant Cemetery, in a grave with other bodies that had been used for medical research. Standing at the spot at last, it comforted her to know that a religious ceremony had been conducted at the time of burial. "At least *someone* had acknowledged this life and death!" she says.

But even this revelation wouldn't entirely lay her father's ghost to rest. And so, on a muggy August day in 1997, at a Presbyterian church in Hamilton, several dozen friends and family gathered to mark the long-ago, still painfully echoing, death. "The thing is, I didn't even like my father," Norma says bluntly. "This ceremony is for us, really." And a gentle, emotional ceremony it was, complete with prayers, hymns, and readings from each surviving member of Norma's family, an eclectic yet profound collection of words by the likes of Victor Frankl, Hannah Arendt, and James Joyce. As she looked out at the crowd and began the service, Rev. Kathy Kraker remarked that we were "a mixed bunch of souls," brought together for a unique occasion. The ceremony included a moment aptly described as "a call to name our brokenness." The words stay with me. If you don't name something, or acknowledge its existence, it's tough, if not impossible, to move beyond it. Although the idea to hold a funeral had welled from Norma's own foundation of sadness, there was also a curious lightness about it, a palpable sense of relief and release.

After completing her B.A., Norma went on to teacher's college, and in the fall of 1998, took a position at an American school in Cairo. Before leaving, she told me: "That funeral really had an effect. It was like this huge burden was lifted off my shoulders, just gone! Others in my family feel the same way. Many good things have happened since then that are hard to explain." Norma had done something essential, something that few did after a suicide back in 1956: faced her grief, the truth about her family, and all its underlying welter of jagged emotion. So many people, like Norma, told me stories of grief denied popping up in the strangest places, at the strangest times. One way or another, it has to come to the surface, or it will wreak havoc in unseen and dangerous ways.

There's a stereotype that situates despair in the alienating blur of cities, but people in rural areas are just as prone to experience it. This is not a joyous time to be trying to eke out an existence from the land. I learned that when I visited the Canadian branch of the Samaritans in Lethbridge, Alberta, which serves virtually the entire province south of Calgary, with its small communities, native reserves, and isolated ranches and farms. Anxious, depressed, and suicidal callers keep the phone lines busy at the Samaritans' distress centre, some of them in genuine acute agony, others suffering more chronic and curious difficulties. On the centre's walls were tacked lists of regular nuisance callers, more than one a "lonely farmer" with some pitiable habit to confess, or secret, raging need to routinely vent at strangers. (A typical note read: "'Bob' wants to talk to female volunteers only, about bestiality.")

Sometimes tragedies happen, even after people in real distress reach out. Two of Hilde Schlosar's volunteers had recently tried to help a man who called after he'd turned on his car in a secluded garage, somewhere on the southern plain. He was already becoming disoriented from the carbon monoxide fumes, and his location was so isolated that the police were unable to find him in time. The horrified volunteers literally heard the man take his last breath. The situation spoke loud and clear of the ambivalence so many suicidal people feel, even as they enact their own deaths—and of the toll suicide can take on people beyond the deceased's family.

If anyone understands these truths, it's people running organizations like the Samaritans, now affiliated with a sister organization called Befrienders International, which seeks to bring distress counselling and suicide prevention services to every country in the world. You might call them experts in global despair management, from the original phone line service that still operates in London, to a huge diversity of culturally specific programs, like puppet theatre in remote Sri Lankan villages and peer counselling in British and North American penitentiaries. It was Hilde who in 1996 had helped launch Canada's first suicide prevention program run entirely by inmates, at Drumheller Institution, tucked away among the dinosaur bones of Alberta's badlands. In 1997, she took me there for a visit.

We arrived at the prison during a lockdown—all prisoners are confined to their cells twenty-three hours a day—that had been instituted because of a recent riot, and were ushered through a sprawling warren of one-storey buildings, security checkpoints, and designated safe areas. In a locked meeting room, Hilde and I talked with four of the twelve inmates who make up the Samaritans group that offers confidential distress counselling to other inmates. The need for such counselling in prisons is hardly new, given their notoriously high suicide rates. Drumheller, a medium-security institution, has one of the lower rates in Canada, but during this riot, said the men, they had been called upon to keep vigil with more than one despairing inmate through long, awful nights.

Wayne Carlson, the group's leader, was motivated by a loss of his own. While imprisoned at Stony Mountain Penitentiary some years earlier in Manitoba, a friend of his named Chris Hood had killed himself, at the age of twenty-eight. "Chris's death could have been prevented," says Carlson. What was lacking for Hood and others like him, he believes, was the presence of people trained to spot someone at risk of attempting suicide, and to effectively intervene in an emotional crisis. Today, when prisoners arrive at Drumheller, they are shown a Samaritans video, produced locally and featuring some of the "Sams" themselves as actors, depicting scenarios in which an inmate might seek help. Names of the Sams are prominently posted throughout the prison. Ordinarily, inmates have freedom of movement during the day, and can approach a Sam themselves, with sessions taking place in cells or meeting rooms. Prisoners in isolation ("the hole") may also request that a guard send in a Sam for a counselling session. During the lockdown, Hilde also debriefed the men on the symptoms of post–traumatic stress syndrome—nightmares, loss of sleep, loss of appetite, feelings of numbness, and disorientation.

Does the program work? "You can't measure prevention," says Hilde, but the Sams are continually evaluating their program, through weekly meetings with each other, and monthly ones with Samaritans staff. They also compile statistical data that are strictly anonymous and confidential. Over time, says Hilde, with the support offered by the Sams to a prison population, "you'd expect the general level of stress to go down, and we do monitor that and consider it important." Three years after the Samaritans got started, they are officially endorsed by the prison administration, and have become known and respected among the inmates, mainly by word of mouth. "Kindness and compassion are lonely entities in prison," says Carlson quietly, as he thumbs through a copy of Chris Hood's suicide note. "I've been in the system a long time, and I know what happens to people. I also know how people respond to kindness, acknowledgement, validation." His sentiments are echoed by the other men, all of whom say they have lost someone to suicide, in and out of prison.

Now in his mid-fifties, Carlson doesn't gloss over his years as a bank robber and rather flamboyant prison escape artist. He is now on a work release and living in a halfway house, working for the Lethbridge Samaritans on furthering their prison programs, and speaking to high school students about the downside of a life of crime. By the time he left prison, he was well on the way to redeeming himself. A talented writer, Carlson gave me some of his work the day I met him during the Drumheller lockdown. I passed it on to the editors of *This Magazine*, who assigned Carlson a piece on his recent experiences and observations of prison life. "Riot," a gritty, at times absurdist essay, was published in the magazine later that year, and won an honourable mention at the National Magazine Awards. We still correspond, and his writing career is well under way, with plans for works of both fiction and nonfiction based on his life experiences, in and beyond "the big house." CBC's *the fifth estate* aired a documentary feature about him and the Samaritans this past February.

Through the eyes of people like Norma Beattie and Wayne Carlson, my own eyes were opened on the matter of how many lives, in so many places, are touched and marked forever by suicide. Where before I might dispassionately read or hear of suicides without a sense of connection, now, when I read a short news item, for instance, about a native reserve that has had ten suicides in the past year, I stop in my tracks. I know this is an emotional apocalypse. I shudder at the thought of such unchecked devastation, some of it irreparable. I know that only ignorance and denial could possibly stop Canadians from viewing the suicide rate in native communities as a national disaster worthy of emergency measures. Among the small number of people, native and non-native, who do turn their attention to the problem, heroism is demanded, burnout is common, and solutions are not easy or obvious. Healing from individual, family, and community trauma echoing through generations has only begun, and will also take generations.

Meanwhile, hollow, sensationalized portrayals routinely show up in film and on TV, leaving a person who's actually been near a real suicide to either cultivate numbness or give in to painful feelings. Careless misunderstandings about the nature of suicide and the experience of survivors show up so often, unbidden. There was, for instance, the wholesale media bitchification of Courtney Love in the months after her husband's death. Reading the sniffy articles casting aspersions on Love for having on-line chats with fans about her feelings at the time, I thought I must be the only human being alive who could entirely forgive her what to others seemed like wallowing. When a Seattle rock group wrote a song that mocked her late husband's death, it was reported that she had gone to visit the band leader, pleading for some understanding. When I read about the callous reply she was said to have received—"If the shoe fits, wear it"—I felt only dismay at the indifference of those who would coldly rebuke someone, even a mouthy rock celebrity, in the face of her immense suffering. "Give her a break," I found myself muttering as I read the news item. "You have no idea what she's going through."

There was something ugly and undeclared in the animus expressed against Love that I think had something to do with envy and sexism, on top of sheer ignorance of the pain that goes with grieving a suicide. She's fierce, intelligent, talented, beautiful, rich, brazen. Is it any wonder some might wish to bring her down with an accusation of murder? Having watched Love weather this storm of mostly male media aggression while moving beyond her grief, having witnessed the unseemly antics of her estranged father, and having read of her firm declaration that her daughter by Cobain "will not be fetishized," I can't help respecting her and feeling a rather protective empathy.

It was the same way I felt toward other strangers suddenly turned suicide survivors whose stories showed up in the news, like Pia Southam, or American author Louise Erdrich, after the suicide of her husband, writer Michael Dorris. When a reporter for *New York* magazine described how he'd arrived unannounced at Erdrich's home, how she'd stood on her porch crying and asking him to please leave her alone, I felt a sense of outrage, and wished I could have been there shooing him off with a broom—though I also noted the irony that the image came courtesy of this man's published article, which I read. And when, after the death of Ted Hughes, a letter to the editor appeared in *The Globe and Mail* declaring that while Hughes might have been an excellent poet, he was obviously a "sleazeball" in his personal life, by virtue of the fact that two wives had killed themselves, I was taken aback by the glibness of the judgment. The fact that Ted Hughes lost two wives to suicide suggests many complex, important things about the psychology of relationships, and of suicide, that might fruitfully be explored, but never will be by those lacking compassion, or the ability to accept life's inevitable ambiguities.

In all of these cases, though, once I'd sorted through the flurry of my own reactions, I settled down and came to my own conclusions: Everyone who goes through such a trauma, famous or not, feels something profound and entirely outside the limited vision of such publicly aired idiocy and voyeurism. These distractions become only part of the whole experience to be endured.

It was a sense of how terrible it would be to grieve a suicide alone that motivated me to train to as a volunteer counsellor in late 1996. The Survivor Support Programme of Metropolitan Toronto is the oldest such service in Canada, and by virtue of the size of the population it serves, also the busiest. After eight sessions of training, sometimes painful—role-playing can bring back memories—with a dozen other aspiring volunteers, some survivors of suicide, some not, I went out for the first time to meet a fellow survivor.

Night begins around 5:30 in Toronto in January, and it's unfor-
givingly cold. I drive through the early darkness into a remote,
unfamiliar suburb of Toronto, a sprawling nowhere-land of low-
cost high-rises, strip-malls, smoky donut shops, muffler-repair
franchises. It is a landscape imbued with all the welcoming charm
of a Siberian gulag. I've got the radio tuned to a station that airs
Dr. Laura Schlesinger nonstop all evening. I must admit, the call-
in advice show is gruesomely fascinating. I even once bought a
remaindered copy of Schlesinger's best-selling *Ten Stupid Things
Women Do To Mess Up Their Lives*, figuring I had probably done
eleven of them. This was during a period when I would sprint
from my office at *Equinox* to the self-help section of the mall
bookstore at lunch. Judging from the author photos on some of
the dust jackets, it seems the first thing those who would help
ourselves should do is bleach our teeth.

But as I listen to Dr. Laura dish out her snarky brand of doctor-
ing, I can't believe how many people, like shameless puppies, want
to elicit this famous stranger's approval, or more often, to present
their waggling rumps for punishment. "Please, Dr. Laura, tell me
how bad I am, and then forgive me . . . ." seems to be the tenor of
most calls. Only on rare occasions does Dr. Laura spare a caller her
waspish wrath—when children phone, or now and then, when
people whose unpolished vulnerability is so powerful, even this arti-
ficial and public situation can't diminish it. "Oh, shut up," I say to
the radio as the diva-doc cuts in with a quip before the caller has
adequately explained her situation. "She said her *ex*-husband," I
mutter. The one thing she does not always do well, I can't help
noticing, is listen. And a counsellor who doesn't listen is sort of like
a pilot who can't fly. Maybe real listening is such a rarity now, attention spans so short, and lives so disconnected, fewer see the difference between canned, scattershot pseudo-wisdom and genuine
response. I turn the radio off and pull into the parking lot of a
forbidding high-rise. For the next hour and a half, what I am called
upon to do, more than anything else, is listen.

In the brightly lit lobby, I meet with my fellow volunteer, Robin, an easy-going and likable guy in his late twenties, who's completing his Master's degree in social work, and whose wife is about to have their second child. He looks dreadfully tired, but still manages to grin and gather his energy for our appointment, when we will listen to and counsel as best we can someone recently bereaved by a suicide. We press the intercom buzzer, the door lock clicks open, and we're on our way, up an elevator and down a long anonymous hallway to our destination: one family's sad, troubled home.

Throughout the city, every week of the year, in private homes and church meeting rooms, people are going two by two into the night, to meet with others who have reached out for help. Most have found out about the program by word of mouth, from a police officer who arrives at the scene of the suicide, a minister, physician, or friend. Marking its twentieth anniversary in 1999, the Survivor Support Programme grew out of a study on bereavement in widows, and began in response to research showing that those who had recently experienced a suicide were at high risk for suicidal feelings themselves, and more likely to act on them than other bereaved groups. Back then, the word "suicide" carried enough stigma not to be included in the program's name; even today, says executive director Karen Letofsky, who has been with the program since the beginning, people appreciate discretion, some requesting that material be sent in unmarked envelopes.

Literally thousands of people have used the service over the years, some driving hundreds of miles to receive this unique specialized counselling that can't be found in their home communities. Mostly people make contact within a few weeks or months of the suicide, but the program has been known to counsel people who are finally grieving suicides that occurred years, even decades, earlier. There is always a waiting list of potential clients to be matched with volunteers, of whom there are at any given time about three dozen.

Letofsky puts much thought into matching volunteers and clients, taking into account the similarity of their experiences. It's part of the program's philosophy to pair as co-counsellors a survivor with a non-survivor. A survivor can easily empathize with specific inner conflicts of a person bereaved by suicide, and signals that it is possible to restore balance and emotional order, enough even to have something left over for someone else. But a non-survivor's presence is important too. It says that grief after suicide need not carry a stigma, that even people who have not directly experienced this kind of loss can offer sympathy, understanding, and support—a link back to the wider community.

Sometimes, says Letofsky, the city's suicides seem to come in unaccountable waves, inundating the list all at once, making the waiting time many months, and causing her to wake up in the night, haunted by the thought of all those people clamouring for help at the worst time of their lives. In twenty years, there has been only one client suicide, and one of a volunteer who was also a survivor. Both events were devastating to staff and volunteers. Yet tragic as these deaths were for all involved, that's a pretty good track record for any helping agency involved in community mental-health care. The model seems sound, providing the choice of not just eight one-on-one sessions with a two-member volunteer team, but also eight sessions of group support with as many as twelve other survivors. Anyone who seems to need extra help is referred to a psychiatrist, psychologist, or other bereavement professional.

A main tenet of this program, and it is key, is that grief is something you pass through, and evolve from; not something you remain within forever. The idea is not to freeze-frame suicide survivors, in their own minds or in the eyes of others, as eternally outside the ken of ordinary existence by virtue of their tragedies. The program establishes a time boundary on counselling that may in some ways be arbitrary—there's no suggestion that someone is magically healed by eight sessions of talk and tears—but also recognizes that it is up to the individual or family to make use of the supports they have in their own network of family, friends, and community. If gaps exist, there's time and space in the counselling sessions to figure out what to do about them.

Eight sessions is enough time to get to know people and their situations reasonably well, to discuss everything from the over-powering feelings of anger, guilt, and confusion to preparing for the tasks, both spiritual and practical, of letting go. At what point does a parent dismantle a beloved son's bedroom after a suicide? What do you say when someone asks how many kids you have? How do you cope with the anger of others, sometimes directed at you, and the way the death changes other relationships in your family? How do you cope with your own anger at the deceased? The questions and issues are profound and numerous, the need to talk about them often urgent, yet usually suppressed in day-to-day living. The sessions become, for many, the safe place where it all gets aired. They can be intensely painful, but also grounding, cathartic, and liberating.

After so many years of shepherding wounded people through this process, Letofsky is reflective and philosophical about what may be gained from it, recognizing that to a large extent, it depends on the individual's or family's state of heart and mind. "Some people just want their lives to return to 'normal' as quickly as possible, and aren't really interested in exploring much about what happened," she says. "I think the people who benefit most from the program are those who see it as an opportunity to face some difficult issues within their families, and that takes a lot of courage. But you know, it is possible to look at what went wrong, and get to a point where you're not blaming yourself. You can see all the things that might have led to the suicide, but know you are not responsible for that person's decision. We want to support people in getting to that point, but we recognize how painful that is."

For my part, I found none of the witnessing easy. Before each session, I would spend at least half an hour sitting quietly, compos-ing myself, donning internal emotional battle fatigues, so that I might feel and project strength to someone I knew was going to need it. I would go over my notes from the previous session, and read the volunteer guide, with its suggestions for the subject of that particular meeting. The conversation could meander, but it helped to have in mind a central path we could always return to, if we ended up hitting a dead end or feeling lost. The other volunteer and I would have already discussed any concerns we had with Karen. Perhaps there were generational differences in the way the suicide was viewed, perhaps children were affected, or conflicts within families had intensified since the death. Perhaps there was a real concern that a person might be at high risk for suicide him or herself. If that was the case, there was no beating around the bush—we had to ask, "Are you feeling suicidal? Have you thought out a plan?" From the answers to these questions, we had to assess how serious the risk was, and report our concern. Fortunately, no one I met ever talked seriously of planning his or her own suicide.

If nothing else, it is the sheer magnitude of the loss experience that makes it useful, if not necessary, to discuss each element, piece by piece, sometimes repeatedly until the reality of it sinks in. I had to respect every person I counselled. I felt they were brave to come forward, yet at times, so breathtakingly vulnerable. More than once, I cried driving home, the words of someone in unbearable pain echoing in my head, sometimes triggering a memory of my own. On occasion, I even woke up in the night after a session, haunted by what I'd heard, saying to myself, "My God, how could anyone go through *that*?" Counselling brought me much humility. Hearing others' stories teaches one lesson unequivocally: You are *not* alone in your suffering.

While it was important to be able to respond articulately to what survivors told us, I came to see that what mattered more than anything was our willingness to be there, listening, not tuning out, judging, or rejecting, not gasping in horror. Our simple presence signalled that it was entirely fine to be saying and feeling these uncomfortable, unfamiliar, yet undeniable things. Sometimes, people asked point-blank, "What brought *you* here?" But more often than not, that was peripheral information, and I never offered it unless asked, or unless the person related a disturbing experience, such as seeing a deceased loved one everywhere, and wondered if they had gone insane. I could assure them they had not by revealing that the same thing had happened to me and many others. It was a way of placing an individual experience in a larger context, but not everyone wanted or needed to do that. We let their concerns lead the discussion, guiding gently when we could. I came to see the role of the volunteer as more than anything that of a human shock absorber, someone who muffled the waves of massive feeling, and kept them from rising and spilling over into an unanswering wilderness. We couldn't take away someone's pain altogether, but we could help ease it for a time, offer a soothing compress on a wounded heart that we understood would take a long time to heal, and would have to do much of its own regeneration to return to a state of healthy functioning.

At the end of these sessions, shaking hands or hugging people I would in all likelihood never see again, I sometimes wondered if we'd managed to do anything at all. It seemed such a small thing to have offered, and sometimes, the people were still so obviously hurt and bewildered. But usually, they thanked us, sent us away with a card summing up their feelings, and sometimes, with small gifts. Fragile though they often seemed in those moments, these were people I recognized were on their way to being survivors. We said goodbye and wished them well.

After that, we could only hope.

STRANGERS ON THE NET

i thought about it long and hard and i am gonna do it . . .
as i sit here crying not understanding why i am so sad

After long hard thought I have also decided to do it. I am
beyond all the crying I just feel numb. Frozen. It's better
than feeling sad

---

when all is said and done the end has truly come

Leave all worthless and vile behind / amidst wide spread
wings bright / I'll give you comfort and delight, / Never a
worry never a fright / Neath my wing you will grow and
know all you once sought / come to me / My Dark Angel

Susan [not her real name] is still unconscious not
responding. i will be back tomorrow to print any
messages to her for her mom to read to her around noon
. . . QT, her ex-husband

People in distress will reach out just about anywhere for help. The
above messages, along with many others, began appearing in my
email box, and in those of subscribers to an international suicide-
prevention discussion group run from Australia on April 2, 1998.
By April 4, "Susan" had reportedly taken an overdose of various
medications. Her ex-husband continued to correspond with a

second apparently suicidal woman, who eventually posted her phone number at his request. Another man requested that Susan's mailing address be forwarded so that everyone could send her cards and gifts to let her know she was loved. Susan's mother had read to Susan the emails of encouragement and sympathy she received. Susan had regained consciousness and was soon to be released from hospital, with expectations of forming relationships with the people who had wished her well, despite the fact that she had never met a single one of them in person.

Some subscribers to the discussion group—distress centre volunteers, social workers, psychiatrists, and others with an interest in the subject—began forwarding Susan the addresses of bona fide on-line crisis counselling services (which this group is not), as well as messages attempting to talk her out of her plans. Others, like "Dark Angel," encouraged her. Still others in the group contacted the on-line manager, alerting him to the situation. He said he would "gently prod" anyone who was suicidal to the appropriate on-line support group, though it's uncertain whether Susan herself would have felt a gentle prod while unconscious. A lively debate ensued, as everyone tried to figure out what did, didn't, should have, or could have happened—and contemplated the brutal irony that a collection of people with a stated interest and in some cases expertise in suicide prevention manifestly failed to prevent an attempted suicide.

It was indeed a creepy feeling, checking my mailbox every day, and regarding the growing suspense of each new installment, like the latest soap opera episode. Who, exactly, is qualified or duty-bound to direct traffic on the information highway, when it looks like someone is about to crash and burn, and what are we to do when we ourselves end up witness or victim in the pileup?

This scenario isn't unique: More and more, suicidal people are finding in the Internet a means of communicating their thoughts and feelings. Why not? There's safety in knowing you are anonymous, though not so entirely that you couldn't be found, in a pinch, if someone in cyberspace read your message and took the trouble to alert authorities who could track you down, which has happened. And anyone who sends out a suicidal message to strangers, even if he or she can't admit it, is asking, and surely hoping, to be saved. "The threats may involve a bit of drama," says my friend Hilde of the Samaritans. The Canadian Samaritans offer only phone–distress counselling, but the British branch of the organization has provided on-line support for people in crisis since 1995. "Suicidal people are feeling so worthless, so powerless, that they want to invoke a response from someone, somewhere. The Internet is an ideal vehicle to get that validation," says Hilde.

Suicide prevention experts still believe that for most people in distress, face-to-face or phone communication is more useful: The connection made is closer for obvious reasons, and it is easier to gauge, through cues of body language or voice, the real severity of the person's risk for suicide. But there may be a small group of people for whom communication via computer is actually more effective—possibly the only way they would communicate their feelings at all. Though the UK Samaritans still receive most of their cries for help over the phone—about 96 percent of their 4.4 million contacts per year—emails from the distressed are on the rise, with 7,300 contacts in 1997.

It's just one issue up for discussion in the new and growing field of "psychotechnology," which studies human behaviour in electronic environments. A recent U.S. conference explored such subjects as "the postmodern self," "the fragmented personality," and "on-line pathology." In the case of the on-line suicide counselling and discussion, a host of moral and ethical implications arise, particularly when well-meaning but entirely amateur Net-surfers start meddling with genuine human desperation. If the case of Susan is anything to go by, we still don't know what is going on.

"It's a serious issue and I have a lot of reservations about it," says Pat Harnish, director of the Toronto Distress Centre, which has yet to provide on-line counselling along with its existing anonymous phone services. But the national Kids Help Phone, based in

Toronto, has added an on-line service to its phone counselling for young people, after a pilot test attracted a significant number of troubled boys who said they would never confide in anyone, except via the anonymity of email or a live, one-on-one chat-room session with a trained counsellor. "The Internet has potential for young people who are shy about reaching out," says Ted Kaiser, manager of on-line services for Kids Help Phone. Apart from an incident in which some girls faked a suicide, which was quickly verified as false, Kaiser says the service is being used responsibly. "The nature of the medium, the fact that you have to sit there and type out a message, and that you get something in writing back, means that it has a calming effect," says Kaiser, noting that that is particularly useful for impulsive teenagers.

People trained in assessing suicide risk among phone callers or electronic help–seekers are at least trying to be sensitive to the unique dynamics of on-line relationships, but now there's a whole other troubling phenomenon on the Net: sites run by people who are in one way or another fascinated by suicide, ranging from the earnest, helpful, and informative to the puerile and repulsive, if not downright dangerous.

Infoseek's search engine pointed me to 172, 657 pages containing the word "suicide." At the 1997 conference of the American Association of Suicidology in Memphis, a Seattle psychiatrist who had studied the Internet estimated a global page total of more than 350,000, likely to keep rising as we hit the millennium, with less than a third devoted to actual suicide prevention. During one cruise, I easily accessed the melancholic musings of Freak, tree, and Burn Worm (not their real names, I suspect), who had made their electronic way, along with dozens of suffering strangers, to the Emotional Repository of Haveaheart's Depression and Suicide Home Page. "My mind is lathered with numerous thoughts" was a typical opener to lengthy discussions of painful childhood memories, relationship breakups, insomnia, ineffective therapists and drugs, and the generally cruel state of the world sensitive souls are forced to inhabit—and often consider leaving by way of suicide. Together, they sank into pits and abysses, listened to the silence scream, brooded in the darkness, and offered each other cyber-hugs, along with poems and song lyrics that were by turns morbidly purple, irritatingly self-indulgent, predictably cynical, and touchingly confused and yearning. Under the liberating cloak of anonymity, Freak, tree, and Burn Worm appeared to take comfort from connecting with others of their gloomy ilk, by way of their distantly scattered computer screens.

Eavesdropping as a journalist on the cyber-conversations of the depressed made me feel a bit like a waitress in a rowdy bar at closing time—the patrons are having a whale of a time, but to a sober outside observer who's spent several hours in their company, they seem so tedious, at times pathetic, if only they knew. Empathy I may have, but couldn't we all just go home and get some sleep?

Thousands of web pages appeal to people interested in the latest speculations about the deaths of Kurt Cobain, Bre-X's Michael de Guzman, and the Heaven's Gate cult members. And many pages further signal the morbid state of pop-cult obsessions, with the self-promotions of musical groups, mostly Goth and industrial, that have discovered a handy formula: Pick a word, any word, slap "suicide" in front of it and voila! Your band has a name. Long live the Suicide Kings, Suicide Commando, Suicide Snowman, Suicide Algebra, and Suicide by Apnea.

Champions of questionable humour include the Cool Ways to Kill Yourself site: "Don't be boring and just take sleeping pills—go out with style and flare!" Suggested debonair deaths for don't-wannabes include falling through chain saws, swallowing Christmas ornaments, chopping your own head off while standing next to a world leader, and death by Seinfeld, which involves having a strong, burly friend beat you to death with Jerry Seinfeld—it sounds more like assisted suicide to me.

It's difficult to know what order of solemnity, faux or otherwise, is intended by alt.suicide.holiday, and difficult to confirm the reported suicide of Fang and others who have left what appear to be suicide notes on the website. You enter by clicking between two human skull icons, and only after reading and agreeing to heed a rather prickly warning: "These pages deal with serious topics of a mature nature. Some users may find the content morally or ethically unpleasant. If you think you are one of these people, please do not proceed further. If you do proceed, you do so by your own choice and agree not to raise any complaints with either the author of these Web pages, or the authors of the work contained here, or the site on which they are stored." The warning is there, presumably, because well-intentioned people have indeed complained about alt.suicide.holiday's content—anything and everything you ever wanted to know about suicide, and notably, chat among what appear to be genuinely suicidal people who do not wish to be talked out of their plans. The site has garnered criticism for publishing a comprehensive suicide Methods File. Here, you can discover the pros and cons of death by way of a range of drugs, from insulin to digitalis, and musings on the merits of dozens of other checkout scenarios. Though it is illegal in most countries to provide and assist a suicidal individual with the actual physical means to kill themselves, publicly disseminating general information of this kind is not. That's why *Final Exit* can be an international bestseller, and why sites like a.s.h. can exist with impunity.

That anyone would be obsessed enough with this subject to compile such a detailed and lengthy list may be disturbing, but upon examination, it appears meant to be mostly humorous, in an aggressive, black, and definitely-not-for-everyone way. There is, for instance, a graphic entry for disembowelment, billed as "trendy for insane martial arts fanatics and gay Japanese poets called Mishima." Despite the juvenile quality of much that appears on alt.suicide.holiday, it does seem to take its mandate as a suicide information source seriously, offering links to support groups for depression and other psychiatric disorders, to on-line counselling provided by the British Samaritans (jo@samaritans.org), and even to sites containing the scholarly musings on suicide and immortality of philosopher David Hume. Hard to say who exactly this is all aimed at, besides angst-ridden undergraduates who have been exposed to too much poetry by Sylvia Plath. I tried several times to access a Personality Test that promised to tell me how I measured up to other a.s.h. visitors, but the site was perpetually inactive. The wisdom of the alt.suicide.holi-day "author" Thomas B. Jones II also shows up as a reverential quote on a Goth site called Dance to the Sound of a Suicide: "When you hate daylight, when you hate anything, you will develop a sort of ambiguity about life and you get reckless in your habits. You overeat. You take dope. You fall in love with a bad person. You declare war against society." I was happy enough to exit alt.suicide.holiday, with its final, foreboding image of a sickle-wielding grim reaper, and the turgidly dispensed advice: Be Not Afraid of What Comes Naturally.

While I may have questioned my own journalistic ethics in peep-ing and reporting on the intensely personal conversations of various support groups (forgiving myself by reasoning that anyone who posts a message must be aware that they are going public on a global scale), I had to seriously review my membership status as a decent human being when I found myself staring at DeathNews—"Takes You Where Living Can't!" It's a "forum on death culture, including downloadable video capture of executions, suicides, mutilations, atrocities, war crimes and other scenes." I didn't make it beyond the preview page, where the two photographic images served up as teasers—a penis being pierced, and what looked like a body with not much of its head still intact—no doubt pale in comparison to the "new, improved Deathloops" I might have sampled.

But don't confuse DeathNews with the ultra-respectable DeathNet, the on-line voice of the Right To Die movement, and winner of numerous awards, including the Canadian Internet Directory's Top Web Site of 1996. The site almost cheerfully espouses "death with dignity" and "self-deliverance." In lovely Deco script, The Art & Science of Suicide offers "the latest how-to liter-ature of suicide." Where the a.s.h. Methods File is predominantly frivolous, this one is deadly serious. As it's all "for mature adults only," you must click verification that you are over the age of twenty-one. I don't know how they would tell the difference between my forty-year-old touch and that of a curious teenager. And since the vast majority of people who commit suicide are well over twenty-one, this seems a gratuitous nod to public responsibility. If this site had audio, it would be New Age synthesizers and harps, or Hooked On Classics Pachabel covers. But for me, no amount of lulling, breathy-voiced aura, tasteful typeface, and mainstream approval can pretty up the consumerist mentality at the heart of all this death talk. What I really want to know is, will I receive an attractive tote bag if I make a purchase at the Life's End Bookstore advertised here?

Still, it's not hard to see why some would question whether any of this is dangerous, after several Net-related suicides. One California teen committed suicide by lying down on railroad tracks, in accordance with information on "Cool Ways to Kill Yourself." The site was bookmarked on his computer, and the downloaded information in his knapsack. In the months after the Heaven's Gate deaths, San Diego distress centres documented one suicide that appeared to be a copycat; there has also been a case of a suicide pact carried out in Canada between a man from Ohio and one from Ontario who met and made their plans via email. But the Electronic Frontier Foundation, an on-line civil liberties group, has criticised the media's simplistic fuelling of fears about the Internet around such cases, taking a classic democratic freedom-of-speech stance, and pointing out that the Internet, in and of itself, does not possess evil powers of mind control, and therefore could not "cause" a suicide. But the issue of who or what is in control, and the ramifications of the Internet for human communication, go deeper and have far more subtle impacts than that position addresses.

It's heartwarming to hear stories of small acts of heroism, like that of the man who alerted police after reading a woman's on-line posting that she'd just taken a lethal dose of pills. And if depressed people who find it difficult to confide in others find comfort and understanding via their computers, could this be a bad thing? In a word, yes. Of course, no one can stop suicidal people from inter-acting with one another on the Internet or anywhere else, though the benefits of on-line peer support may on occasion be outweighed by the downside of fuelling each other in the tunnel vision that typically characterizes the suicidal state. Issues of addic-tion and dependancy also come into play. A person who already feels painfully isolated may only be driven further inward by the handy keyboard and its at times questionable electronic solace. And in the case of someone other than a trained counsellor in a controlled setting, there's something both naive and grandiose about seeking to "help" a suicidal person by getting to know them on-line and even meeting them in person. The case of Susan illus-trates this problem. It goes against every tenet of modern distress counselling, which always maintains anonymity, and offers help from people who know what actually constitutes help. "If we were to trace calls on everyone who expressed suicidal ideation, people would very quickly stop calling us," points out Hilde, of the Samaritan phone services. She suggests the same is true for people using the Internet. "Most people still want to retain the power to decide. They choose this anonymous form of disclosure because there are no strings attached and no interference."

The Net may have saved lives, but it can also deceive, cheapen, and commodify. There were certain websites that I could not enter without having to crack out my VISA card. As we make judgments, we must also beware hypocrisy. Tasteful DeathNet receives main-stream design awards, while the more crudely executed alt.suicide.holiday is easily scorned. Yet some of the lethal recipes each site makes available are the same, and like the disturbing DeathNews, DeathNet wants my VISA number, adding new mean-ing to the expression "shop till you drop."

The Net draws people together around their obsessions or ailments, but when the subject is as profound and complex as suicide, it may have serious drawbacks in addressing them. Experts advise that if in the course of your Internet wanderings you stumble upon someone you believe to be suicidal, it's wise to compassionately direct him or her to seek help from trained people, on- and off-line—don't try to play God. "We can't save the world. We can't save anybody," says Hilde philosophically. "All we can do is help someone save themselves."

It's good advice, and I thought about it as I explored the Internet myself. Along with joining an on-line discussion of suicide prevention, I also subscribed to an on-line suicide-survivor support group. I never made my presence known by formally introducing myself, though a single electronic message would have ended up in the mailboxes of however many members there were at the time scattered throughout the English-speaking world. Instead I simply read the mail that landed in my chunk of cyberspace. It amounted mostly to a cosy conversation among a few veteran members, and the tentative words of the newly bereaved looking for somewhere to turn in their confusion and, in some cases, desperation. It was not uncommon to open my email box each day and find messages like this: "Hi, my name is Mary Doe. Two months ago, my husband shot himself, and since then, my life has been a nightmare. I don't know what to do, no one seems to understand, and so I thought I would try this group." In response would come a cluster of sincere messages of support. I only ever responded once to an individual, and even then, I opted to maintain privacy and sent my response to her plea, which resonated deeply with my own experience, to her email address only. I have no idea whether she received it, as I never got an answer. I suspect my message was one of many.

Sometimes new voices would join in, and confess that they had been lurking on-line for months, reading messages but not participating, until someone wrote something that moved them to finally take the plunge and reveal their presence. I can only assume there were also others out there who preferred to remain unseen, gaining something in the way of insight or comfort from words aimed at others yet applicable to them. Evidently, I was not the only one who was reluctant to go public in this forum. Why the reticence?

For me, it stemmed partly from a vague discomfort with the assumption of virtual, instant intimacy among strangers. Was this not potentially overwhelming, or purely voyeuristic? How could you not want to respond helpfully to all those people with their pain bursting forth on your screen, yet how could any one person adequately do so? What level of emotional responsibility do people assume when they take it upon themselves to reach out and randomly touch someone in cyberspace?

The technology may be new, but the dilemma it poses for human interaction is ancient. The words we use to describe ourselves and our experiences are not literally *us*, but it seems easy to forget that when the electronic tools of would-be communion are so readily at hand. Some people express themselves in writing better than others—what you see on the screen is not necessarily what you'd get in person, and someone who is not adept at written communication may be at a disadvantage, or even unwittingly destructive, in the context of computerized communication. Can all that you might intuit from taking in a person's physical presence—from hearing a voice or looking someone in the eye—really be divined through an accumulated cluster of typed words? If the answer is no, and I believe it is, then just how useful is this electronic emotional stroking? As I also learned the hardest way, even in a live, intimate, flesh-and-blood relationship, it is difficult enough to understand another person's inner life, to know his truth, much as we might wish we could, or imagine we do.

Most of the on-line participants probably had the capacity to place their activity in perspective. There was some genuine information-sharing, some giving and receiving of support that didn't seem out of proportion. Yet the fact that so many flock to their computer keyboards in search of connection says something rather sad about the isolating tendencies of the real world. If grief were more acceptable to express, if more people knew how to respond to and allow for it as a matter of course, the bereaved would not feel so driven to marginalize themselves, risking distortion and prolongation of their sorrow.

For beyond these issues, my hesitation to participate, and my decision after a couple of months to "unsubscribe" from the group, also had to do with a waning sense of identification, three years after my own tragic loss, with these unfortunate people in the thick of fresh grief. I was beginning to establish boundaries between myself and the intensity of early bereavement—something I had to do, yet always recognized was a delicate balancing act. One woman in the on-line group diligently and publicly welcomed each newcomer, prefacing every message with an account of her loss, which had occurred more than a decade earlier. Reading this repetitive message, I confess to wondering why she didn't send her stock response privately to each novitiate sufferer, sparing others its almost daily reappearance in their emailboxes. I became uneasy with the way this individual so routinely bustled to the rescue, the rote manner with which she trotted out her mourner's credentials. What personal satisfaction did she derive from this? Wounded healers don't like to admit it, but there are some gains to be had in giving. Acknowledging these boosts to one's self-worth, the void of a person's unexamined inner conflicts these activities can fill, is more honest than imagining that any mortal can or should be a nonstop pouring faucet of saintly beneficence. Anyone who denies it's draining to open yourself to multiple griefs is delusional, or has hardened to a point that is anything but saintly, and probably unhelpful.

Altruism can indeed mask narcissism. It's one thing to offer genuine empathy, and to do so from a position of strength that you have reached in resolving your own grief to the best of your capacities. Then, you have something to share beyond sorrow. It's quite another to hide out in the company of the bereaved, searching their faces, or email messages, solely for mirror reflections of your own. If listening to another person express grief becomes merely a jumping-off point for talking about yours ("Oh, yes, I know what you mean. It's just like when I . . ."), then you are in no position to truly help someone, and the only mirror you should be looking into for the time being is your own. Karen Letofsky has had to let go of a few volunteers over the years, whose idea of helping others was telling them what to do or feel, and who in some cases badgered either the survivors they were supposed to counsel, or their fellow volunteers.

I had to ask, as I contemplated this daily flow of suicide-survivor cyber-chat, is there not a danger, in the support group that never ends, of becoming addicted to the vicarious thrill of breaking another's fall, or to the sensation of falling and being caught? Why close the wounds when it feels so good, and is so easy, to keep them open? At what point do the tools of support turn into the crutches of collectively nurtured long-term disability? These issues apply far beyond on-line support groups, and need to be seriously addressed by the survivor movement and those in the field of bereavement counselling.

Surviving a tragic experience may mark and change you, sometimes profoundly, but is it not limiting to make it a predominant badge of identity? It's taken a long time to get here, but I now think of my own survivor state in the same way I view my greying hair, or my right elbow, weakened when I dislocated it in a fall ten years ago—simply realities to be lived with, alterations, rather than complete transformations, in the self I was before these changes or events occurred. Just the way it is. I've been known to do something about the hair; weight training has strengthened the elbow; much soul searching, and simple time, have made Daniel's suicide recede, finally, to a less central position in my life.

There is one other thing I now know. Beyond the support groups, on- or off-line, beyond the grief counselling and psychotherapy, the hand-holding, the sharing of tears and mutual mining of our experiences, beyond the conferences and workshops, beyond the reading and writing of any number of articles and books, there is for every mourner a dimension of grief that is inviolably private, mysterious, unique as a fingerprint, literally beyond words. This is what I remind others, and myself, when I'm asked, do I not feel exposed, writing a book like this? (The honest answer is yes, sometimes.) We can gather strength by standing together to "name our brokenness," as Norma Beattie instinctively knew, but it is in moments of silence and solitude that the essence of our loss is most powerfully revealed. In facing grief, as with death itself, there comes a point when each one of us must inexorably go it alone. If we have been well and truly supported, we will have the strength to endure it.

And in doing so, become more than survivors.

LAST WORDS

JANUARY 1997. I AM WAITING IN LETHBRIDGE to hear whether I will be allowed to interview the Sams at the Drumheller Institution about their suicide-prevention work, even though the prison is in post-riot lockdown. In the meantime, Hilde tells me that there is to be a sweat lodge ceremony at an addiction treatment centre in nearby Cardston, led by a Blackfoot elder, Art Calling Last. He also leads ceremonies and counsels native inmates at the Lethbridge jail. The sweat is held on the third Friday of every month, and is open to guests, non-natives included. Hilde had gone herself some months earlier and encourages me to accompany one of her staff members, Orville Powder. A Métis from northern Alberta, and a former inmate and addict himself who had been involved with training the Sams at Drumheller, Orville regularly attended Calling Last's sweats and other ceremonies. "I think you could use it," he says, teasingly. He has been telling me since I arrived that I am "too serious," and seems to see it as his personal mission to make me laugh. As it happens, my visit to the prison is postponed a few days, so I agree to go to the Cardston ceremony the following day.

On the way there, we pick up his teenage brother, Floyd, who sits shyly in the back seat of Orville's Jeep, speaking up only to complain when he gets tired of listening to his brother's tape selection, mostly powwow drumming and singing. "Put on The Doors, man," he pleads. So it is to the sounds of "Light My Fire" and "Break on Through" that we travel to the sweat, along roads that head straight into southern Alberta's Rocky Mountain foothills, grand and beautiful in the distance under the big blue sky of a clear winter day.

The idea of spiritual cleansing and healing through intense trial makes sense to me. It lies at the heart of most religious mysticism, though rituals of enactment are few and far between for most people in contemporary cultures. I've been drawn to native spirituality in the past, wary at the same time of the white wannabe syndrome. I've avoided the kind of New Age pseudo-native events offered in the city, feeling I would rather wait to be invited to a sweat, when the time seemed right, and the ceremony genuine. Now I feel excitement and anticipation, but also apprehension. I have been told of the power of this experience I am about to undergo. It's not to be taken lightly, and I know I must prepare myself psychologically somehow. Hilde and Orville advise me on what to expect. If the heat gets unbearable at any time, I should bend my head forward to the ground, where the rising air is slightly less intense. Orville says try not to panic, he's seen people scream and freak out and try to blast through the door flap before a round of praying and singing is over. Such reactions are frowned upon as obviously disruptive to the other participants and the spirits summoned through the songs and prayers. "Just stay calm and wait till they open the door at the end of the round," he says. "You don't have to go back in if you don't want to." He fills me in on other small protocols, and I feel as ready as I am ever going to be.

We arrive and change our clothes for the sweat in the nearby centre's washrooms—shorts for the men, loose gowns or long knee-covering T-shirts for the women. Several hundred yards away on the building's flat grounds, the lodge looks tiny, a waist-high, tear-shaped mound. We approach it through the snow, shivering in the January air, past the people tending the fire heating the rocks to be used in the ceremony. Floyd is helping out. ("I can't go in there," he says, looking over at the lodge. "It's too scary.") We step out of our boots, and after waving smoke onto ourselves from sweetgrass burning in a bowl on the ground, crouch to enter the lodge, Orville taking his place beside the seven men already on one side, and Calling Last, back and centre. I crawl in and join the four women seated cross-legged on the other side. We're a mix of natives and non-natives. Only one other man and I have never been to a sweat before.

There are formal introductions around the circle, and ritual offerings of food and tobacco presented to animal and ancestral spirits. The passage into the lodge is secured shut. We sit in the dark now, the rocks steaming and hissing as water is sprinkled on them. The close air is heavy with cedar, sage, and sweetgrass smoke. Orange sparks rise from the rocks in the centre and dance momentarily in the rich, utter blackness as the elder begins the songs and prayers for the first of four rounds. Everyone joins in.

We're to call on the spirits, our ancestors, to come to us in this time and space. I try to quash ironic thoughts about what my good Protestant Irish grand- and great-grandparents would make of this, whether they'd particularly want to come, whether I would want them to. I concentrate on my mother and other dead relatives I loved and hope for the best. The leap into this unfamiliar world happens so fast—like sitting in an airplane wearing a parachute, confident that you understand what you are about to do, then being overcome with blind terror as the door opens onto the sky, and you realize that you must actually jump into it.

The unknown. One moment, I am calmly acclimatizing to strange sensations, sounds, smells, and the tight, hot space in which I cannot see an inch in front of me, and cannot leave until someone or something says it's time. Then, within what seems like seconds of singing along in the dark, a horrible, claustrophobic panic sets in, and my heart beats rapidly, making me breathless. My mind tells me this is impossible, I must *get out*. Now I understand what Hilde and Orville warned me about. I cannot imagine how I will sit here for the next twenty minutes, or however long it is, for I don't actually know. I contemplate the freedom I normally take for granted, the way I am used to doing whatever I want with my body and mind, moment to familiar, unchallenged moment. Briefly, I see myself as some maddened feral creature, furiously digging up the earth with my paws at the edge of the lodge behind me, desperately clawing my way out to safety and blessedly fresh, cool air. This desperation is followed by an immense urge to cower, to cosy up to the shoulder of the person next to me, already as close to me as humanly possible, and whimper. I feel ridiculous even having such impulses.

But something carries me through these moments of primal fear. For once, I don't have to understand; I just know that something real and uplifting is taking place. I can accept that here, my reasoning brain represents only a small part of myself. I must trust in and rely on something other than that. I must acknowledge greater connections to the universe, those parts of myself I ignore most of the time, the ones I can't see or control or understand. Somehow, I fend off my instinct to cringe and flee. I bend my head back and resolve to open myself, to surrender to this unfamiliar spiritual territory, to breathe through my panic. Tears mingle with sweat on my face as new sounds pour from me. I try to absorb the strength and spirit of the others, to kindle some faith that if they can get through this, so can I.

Now I feel an extraordinary shifting of inner forces. It's as though this fear is some large, tough weed that has rooted tenaciously in the depths of my being, choking off the other things that want to grow there. Sitting with my head back, calling to the spirits, I feel this overpowering, clogging thing being pulled up from the centre of my body, up through it, out my open throat.

Then it's gone.

MOIRA FARR

I can't quite believe it. I simply do not feel fear anymore. I'm almost giddy with relief and surprise. By the time the round ends and someone outside opens the flap to let in the pale light and cold air, I have become so immersed in the rhythms of the singing and praying that I am amazed at how much time has gone by. I feel fine, wonderful. I know I will make it through the next rounds, though I still can't quite grasp how I passed from animal terror to this serenity so quickly. I don't want to be too cocky about it, so I sit silently, reminding myself that the next rounds will be even hotter. Everyone is quietly friendly. We lounge around, stretch, and rest ourselves, as new heated rocks are brought to the inner circle.

Orville had told Calling Last that he was bringing someone, and the elder has in turn told some people here. One woman turns and says, "I hear you're a writer from Toronto?" Turns out she is originally from there. She mentions the name of someone, a writer she knows there, but I've never heard of him. She continues, talking about stables and equestrian events. I gradually realize that she thinks I am a *rider*—this is ranch country after all. One of the men in the group is a former rodeo champion who runs a nearby horse and cattle ranch with his wife. She is also participating in the sweat today, graciously filling me in on the meaning of various parts of the ceremony. So finally I say, no, no, I'm a *writer*, and everyone laughs at the mistake. The easy shift from solemnity to irreverence makes the whole atmosphere even less intimidating.

We carry on through three more rounds. There are other intense moments, moments when I do have to put my head to the ground to avoid being overcome by the heat, and the emotions. But it's also exhilarating. Other things happen in there, difficult to explain, sacred. A lightness of spirit, a good, calm energy, runs through all of us as we finish and emerge to change back into our regular clothes, our regular selves. I sleep peacefully that night back at my friend's place in Calgary. When I wake up the next morning, I can still smell the sweetgrass in my hair.

I've thought a lot about the ceremony since then. Somehow, it seems to have hit me in the same unfamiliar places that my grief did, made manifest things I was discovering about myself anyway, over the long haul of surviving, realizing that in a strange way, grief has made me whole, has pierced me in the larger part of myself I have kept buried. I have had to call on this part in order to survive Daniel's death. I've had to dig beneath the surface of myself to find the resources, the intangible, to cope. I am thankful I found what I needed. I have had to bring to the light things about myself I didn't like much as well. So, my wound, paradoxically, is healing me. That larger part of myself I barely knew was there is keeping me alive. I am learning that it is indeed possible to survive anything, and not only survive, but flourish and thrive, as others have done, through life's multitude of tragedies.

These truths are only things I can try to keep reminding myself of, things I do not always remember. I understand how it is for those who give up, how unbearable certain moments can seem. To get through such moments, the only thing we can do is forgive ourselves, and others, for being human; to "name our brokenness," and learn to pick up the pieces—again and again—and, like Sisyphus, to keep shoving the boulder up the mountain.

Three years after Daniel's suicide, I felt I was beginning to feel and acknowledge a distinct moving away from my intense bond with that event.

June 1997. Sitting on the patio of "the Dip" on College Street, having coffee with Tony Burgess, writer, former drug addict, and a man with a delightfully bizarre sense of humour. I first met Tony in the summer of 1993, when he and Lynn Crosbie came over for dinner one evening at Daniel's. I liked him immediately, and the night passed with lots of joking and laughter. But there were pains and problems lurking beneath the cheerful camaraderie—for all of us, I guess. Not long after, in the fall, Tony went back to the drugs he had tried to kick, and nearly died of an overdose. He was alive only because a compassionate passerby called for an ambulance when he found him out cold on the street.

He fully intended to die, Tony tells me later, and it was not his first attempt. He had spent years in and out of various institutions, being diagnosed with a host of mental illnesses and character defects. He had led a restless life travelling the country, never really settling anywhere, getting into lots of trouble, a brilliant mind out of control most of the time, the creativity under wraps of chaos. After his 1993 suicide attempt, he spent months in intensive detox and recovery.

Few of us knew about all this until much later, when Tony was up and about again, clean of drugs and counselling others going through ordeals similar to his own. In the summer after Daniel's death, Tony rented an office beside mine in the building at the corner of Euclid and College. He began working on some fiction. Occasionally he would wander over and knock on my door, and we'd sit and talk about our work, Daniel, addiction, the mysterious workings of brain chemistry. Tony would usually end up making me laugh. The work he began there has since been published in a trilogy of eccentric and poetic novels: *The Hellmouths of Bewdley, Pontypool Changes Everything,* and *Caesarea.* They've been received well critically; Bruce McDonald, of *Hard Core Logo* fame, has bought the film rights for *Pontypool,* intending to make "the great Canadian zombie movie." Tony appears to have conquered something with his last suicide attempt once and for all, something he doesn't want to, or have to, revisit. He and Lynn have since split, but remain good friends. He is in another relationship now, with a woman whose career as a criminal lawyer has taken them both to live in the community of Wasaga Beach, edging into cottage country due north of Toronto.

Back in the summer of 1997, *The Hellmouths of Bewdley* had just been published to good reviews. Tony hadn't yet moved from the city, and seemed to be just getting used to writing seriously, without recourse to substances other than his own very active imagination.

It was good to see how much things were looking up for him, the infectious hope he had, for his writing, for his personal future.

Again, we're laughing. A reporter from the small town of Port Hope, near the village of Bewdley northeast of Toronto, where there is not a large audience for avant-garde fiction, has gotten wind of the book. He called Tony to ask whether he had set his stories in Bewdley for any particular reason. "We in Port Hope always thought that a circus freak show decided to settle there," he said. Tony had not anticipated consternation among Bewdlians over his fictional portrayal of their town, nor for that matter to be made an honorary citizen. Over coffee, he rumbled with laughter wondering if he should avoid the place, for fear of lynching.

The book weaves eerie, shocking tales of life in and around the fictional town, and there are graphic scenes involving suicide, written with such terrible clarity, you know they could only be based on the real experience of the person writing them. Tony told me that his father finally summoned the courage to open this book his son had written, this book that must seem to him so strange and difficult. Over the phone, his father had told him, "I read some of the stories, son, but parts of it I can't. But I want you to know, I am proud of you." I feel tears welling in my eyes at this. "That is wonderful, Tony, I am so happy for you," I say, and mean it. Of course, I find the image moving, of a father bravely tackling the creation of a son he doesn't necessarily understand, yet loves nonetheless. In describing his family background, Tony had once said, "Sure, it was dysfunctional, the usual stuff, but I don't blame my family for my problems—I always gave worse than I got." But I also know that I want to cry because I wish it was Daniel sitting across from me recounting all of this. I wish it was Daniel telling me he had heard his father say those words.

I ask Tony to inscribe my copy of *Hellmouths*, and when I get home I read what he has written: "To Moira, who knows that a hellmouth can also be breathed through." I treasure it. Now, Tony and I email each other occasionally. He is busy on his latest novel, in a home work space he calls a "nest," on a riverside property where he can catch fish off the dock. Last spring, he played Curly in a production of *Oklahoma!* at the local little theatre. "Outrageous fun," he says. "I've never worked harder in my life!"

Fun. By the summer of 1997, after several years of turning my attention toward the tragic in life, I begin to see messages everywhere to lighten up. I could identify with Spalding Gray's self-styled protagonist in *Monster in A Box,* endlessly working, incapable of truly relaxing until he'd grappled with every last mysterious complexity, even titling his monstrous manuscript *Impossible Vacation.* When the editor of *Seasons,* the magazine of the Ontario Federation of Naturalists, calls to ask if I would like to spend ten days in the province's remote Polar Bear Provincial Park and write an article about it, my first impulse is to turn her down. Too much work to do on the book. But I stop in mid-"it's impossible." When would I ever get such an amazing opportunity again? And so I agree to go and write about this incredible, untouched place, including its polar bears. I get to view a group of them from behind a bit of willow scrub on the tundra, as they lounge on the austere coast of Hudson's Bay, waiting for the ice to form again so they can return to their winter seal hunt. Thousands of geese and other birds fly over us and the vast, magnificent landscape.

As a direct result of this trip I nearly talked myself out of taking, I am now in a relationship, with the photographer assigned to the same story, and have moved to a new city. Different partner, different life. We live near the Ottawa River, and I can leave my back door and run along pathways that trace its banks every day, clearing my head before and after writing. The balance of urban and wild here, the better air, sits well with me. We go birdwatching together; thanks to this man, I now know the difference between a semipalmated plover, a kildeer, a lesser yellowlegs, and a least sandpiper. An accomplished naturalist, he can identify birds by their distant calls; spot at a glance tiny, jewel-like beetles sitting in sleek emerald splendour on forest leaves; stand by the side of a secluded road at midnight and call a barred owl out of the bush as it flaps to a perch above our heads and stares down at us with its brown saucer eyes. He'll stop the car to examine a snake coiling along the pavement. He'll pull the telescope out of the trunk to let me get a better view of the indigo bunting he saw flit through the roadside greenery, or a family of hooded mergansers floating lazily in a reed-filled marsh.

The key to his supreme enjoyment of life seems to be that he can see what is going on, *really* going on around him, in whatever natural place he happens to be. Where others might plod obliviously past all these small natural phenomena, he delights in teeming, fascinating life wherever he finds it, and stops to examine and savour it until he has exhausted his curiosity—till he's had a new experience, knows something he didn't know before. When the inevitable question of suicide came up as we were getting to know each other, his eyes widened and he shook his head. "I just cannot imagine doing that," he said. "I mean, never in a million years."

Good answer.

Later, when I was packing up my things to move to Ottawa, sorting through piles of personal papers and things to file for research, I stopped to reread an essay sent to me by my friend, writer M. T. Kelly, a year after Daniel's death. It's called "A Canoeist's Thoughts in February," and he had sent it to me after I had taken a canoe trip in northern Ontario with a group called Wild Women Expeditions the previous summer. At the top of it he wrote: "Dear Moira: Best as always in this cold and hard winter; and on your wild woman journeys." It's a piece about patience, endurance, and keeping vigil, through memories and in anticipation of future experiences. It discusses how canoeists, like gardeners perusing their seed catalogues as they dream by winter fires, become lost in the contours of maps, in thoughts of future trips on beautiful summer waterways. And it ends with a quote from *The Jesuit Relations*, by one of the seventeenth-century priests who came to the New World to convert the heathen, and found that the heathen had a thing or two to teach them about survival. The priest reported that when he was ill, depressed, suffering from "what an earlier time would call a black night of the soul," the Montagnais (now the Innu) told him:

> Do not be sad; if thou are sad, thou wilt become still worse; if thy sickness increases, thou wilt die. See what a beautiful country this is; *love it*; if thou lovest it, thou wilt take pleasure in it, and if thou takest pleasure in it thou wilt become cheerful, and if thou art cheerful thou wilt truly live.

One crisp late afternoon in autumn, walking along a cottage road in Quebec with my new partner, he points up to the sky. Two ravens spiral against the brilliant blue. "They're playing," he tells me, like a patient tour guide to an overly earnest alien. I watch the big black birds swooping through the sky, diving down, flying up to each other, touching beaks and gliding away, looping back together again slow moments later, on another current of air. It's hard to imagine what the purpose of it all might be except sheer pleasure.

In the winter of 1998, the ice storm that severely crippled eastern Ontario left my companion homeless for more than two weeks. I thought some fun was in order, and so we went to a performance of Slava's SNOWSHOW, featuring the renowned Russian clown Slava Palunin, at the Princess of Wales theatre in Toronto. As the show begins, Palunin shuffles onto the stage holding a long rope that he seems to be fashioning into a noose. Great, I can't help thinking. But the clown does not hang himself. Instead, another odd figure is tugging at the other end of the rope, a figure who through a mimed, comic exchange, turns the first clown's attentions away from the self-destructive things he might do with the rope. Later, in the show's powerful climax, the little clown is flattened and nearly vanquished in a vicious snowstorm, brought to theatrical life with glaring lights, pounding music, and a seemingly endless flurry of small white paper "snow" squares blasting off the stage and from the ceiling, blanketing the audience and the players. When the storm finally ends, and the clown rises again, it seems like the natural end of the performance, but there is more. Suddenly, gigantic multicoloured balls the size of Volkswagens bounce out from the stage and float slowly and majestically over the heads of the audience, who are still shaking snow squares from their hair and clothing. Long after the show ends, many stay standing at their seats, their heads upturned as they bat the huge balls back and forth to each other all over the theatre.

Only a true grinch would not get caught up in the silly spirit of it all, and the normally subdued Torontonians here, young and old, are having one whale of a time, their faces animated with the thrill of this impromptu game. Walking out of the theatre, I can't help smiling at the conservatively dressed older man who probably spends most of his time doing something Toronto-ish like managing investment portfolios, as he beams away himself, unaware that several squares of white paper are still nestled in his thinning hair.

Despite the melancholy caste of many of Palunin's comic tableaux, the show imparts an affirming message: Life may be absurd, you may be clownishly up against the odds on many occasions, but you might as well stick around. You never know when giant balls will descend from the heavens, a gift of simple, joyous play. In this sense, Palunin's clown reminds me of Camus's version of Sisyphus, the rebellious mortal "accused of a certain levity toward the gods," the absurd hero, the man who manages to find happiness even as he descends the mountain to begin the task of pushing his boulder to the top all over again. "A moment comes when the creation ceases to be taken tragically; it is merely taken seriously," concludes Camus. "Then man is concerned with hope."

Right now, it doesn't seem so difficult for me to concern myself with hope. But I suspect that suicide and its related issues will never be far from my consciousness. Shortly after moving to Ottawa, I sat in a chair in my finally unpacked new living room reading a newspaper article about a man who dramatically shot himself on a California freeway. Onlookers gawked and a local television station captured it all on video. The name of the man was Daniel Jones. In the early months after Daniel's suicide, reading such a thing would have caused me agony, might even have made me question my own sanity and feel a grim paranoia about the perversely destined nature of the universe. Now, the coincidence merely rattled me momentarily.

Another recent item that caught my eye was a letter to the editor of the *Ottawa Citizen* from a young man who had gone to a hospital emergency ward suffering acute pain from a chronic illness. The physician on duty told him curtly that he should either learn to live with the pain or commit suicide. I felt the blood rising to my face as I read of this callousness, so illustrative of the ignorance about suicide, so unacceptable from someone who is supposed to be devoting his life to healing people, not adding to their suffering.

I am building a life here, reconnecting with friends who moved to Ottawa years ago, friends I was never able to see much before. One, Kathleen, now a mother of two boys, is a singer-songwriter, and a music therapist. Her clients have included everyone from elderly people with Alzheimer disease to children with cerebral palsy. Now and then, she sneaks away to a recording studio, and hopes to soon have enough material for a CD. I laugh when she tells me that she is in the middle of putting to music—blues, of course—Dorothy Parker's famous poems, including her quintessential take on suicide and the futility of life:

Razors pain you; Rivers are damp;
Acids stain you; And drugs cause cramp;
Guns aren't lawful; Nooses give;
Gas smells awful; You might as well live.

August 1994. A happy memory. Daniel and I are visiting my sister and another close friend in London, England. It is Daniel's first time overseas, and it's fun to be showing him around, exploring the city. We take leisurely walks up Hampstead Heath, through Highgate Cemetery, where a group of Korean tourists are laying long-stemmed red carnations on Karl Marx's grave. From my sister's place in the east end, we board a double-decker red bus each day and wind our way into the centre of the city, wandering in and out of the used-book stores, buying a paisley shirt for Daniel on Carnaby Street, taking his picture outside a boutique called OBSES-SIONS—the title of his first published novel. When we get to the British Museum Library, I can practically feel Daniel's pulse quickening. For a book lover, this is heaven. Its shelves groan with historical treasures, its floorboards trod on through time by so many illustrious figures that it would be hard to keep track of them all. In row upon row of glass cases, gems of literary culture have been placed on view, manuscripts of famous works, from Milton's *Paradise Lost* and the novels of Jane Austen and the Brontës to paper napkins bearing the original scrawled lyrics of Beatles' songs. There are illuminated medieval texts, the Gutenberg Bible, children's classics, exquisitely designed ancient texts in Arabic and Chinese and other languages—it is possible to spend days here browsing, thoroughly engrossed. We do spend hours wandering from case to case, our heads touching as we bend to peer into them. Daniel is silently and completely fascinated. Eventually I leave him and head to the museum. When I return, he is just as calmly engaged as when I left. Finally, he realizes he can't take it all in at once and wrests himself away. "We have to come back," he says. "Soon."

Later that night, he flops back on the fold-out sofa in my sister's living room, puts his hands behind his head, sighs, and looks at me with an expression of amazement. "I'm happy," he says, as though he cannot quite believe it is true. "Just happy." It is wonderful to see him enjoying himself so much, so shockingly rare, by his own account, for him to feel such simple pleasure in being alive. It did not last, of course, and throughout the fall and into the winter I watched him return to the state of guilty self-recrimination, as though he felt that deep down he really did not deserve to feel any joy, and must banish it as quickly as possible, lest anyone get wind of the fact that he, Daniel Jones, loathsome human being, was blessed with a momentary peace of mind, a sliver of grace.

But serene he was then. Near the end of our trip, we had dinner at the home of other friends, Jan and Keith. Jan and I were both celebrating birthdays. The evening ranged from intense and heated literary debate to utter silliness. I took a picture of Daniel taking a picture of Jan; he is leaning back in his chair, his head tilted back. He wears the mirthful, mouth-open, eyes-crinkled-up expression of someone heartily laughing. I see that I have caught behind him part of the shiny birthday banner that Jan has garlanded across the back wall of her dining room—the word HAPPY hangs suspended right over his head. Of all the snapshots I give to his mother after his death, this is the one she frames and places on a shelf in her kitchen.

It is natural, and necessary, to want to salvage something from the wreckage of a loved one's death by suicide. You want to find a way to remember the good times without drowning in memories of the person's bad end. In April 1994, two months after Daniel's death, I returned to my sister's home in London for a week, to retreat and try to regain some of my bearings. It was difficult retracing the journey I'd taken in Daniel's company only eight months earlier; to stand in the same airport where my sister's friend Jo had seen us off, and Daniel had hugged her and we'd all laughed and he'd said to her, "Friends forever, right?" It was painful to sleep alone on the same sofa where Daniel had proclaimed his happiness, to board the double-decker bus and sit in silence as it lumbered into the centre of London, recalling how happy I'd been myself the last time I was here.

I walk with a stride more resolute than I feel toward the museum and into the library. The fact is, I like it here myself, liked it before I brought Daniel here, and want to see it one last time before all the books are moved to a new building, amid much controversy. While it may be more conducive to preserving books and manuscripts, a new building.can never have the character of the old library. As I walk through, peering in the cases once more, recalling Daniel beside me, I feel as though I am doing this on his behalf. For myself, I am struggling to keep a good memory good.

Now, I can retrieve other memories without feeling overwhelmed with the weight of my sorrow. Of course, I am sorry that Daniel had so few genuinely happy and peaceful moments in his life. But I am glad that I was there to share at least some of those rare good times with him.

I am not sorry to have known Daniel Jones. Perhaps, as my friend Laima said, we hurt each other just by being alive and different, but I think we teach each other by virtue of our existence too. I cannot pretend that Daniel's dark side, and his suicide, did not and does not trouble me greatly. Not everyone saw the compassionate, deeply tender, and vulnerable side of this man. I feel honoured that I did, and am now able to say such a thing comfortably in the past tense.

Daniel is dead. I accept that. It is not something that can ever be undone. As the poet James Fenton speculates about his dead friend in the breathtaking poem "For Andrew Wood" in his collection entitled *Out of Danger,* I don't think Daniel would "have us forever howling," or want us to "waste quite away in sorrow." I think about what he has lost, and I look to his own writing:

> That last morning I spent with Assa, I locked the door to her studio as she had instructed. I walked down the wooden staircase at the side of the garage where her studio was. It was the first day of spring, and water poured from the eavestroughs on the side of the garage and onto the snow, which had mostly melted. I walked up Major Street

to Bloor and sat in a doughnut shop drinking coffee until the taverns opened. It was my twenty-first birthday.

I drank beer all day. In the early evening I walked down Major Street and stood at the end of the driveway leading to Assa's studio. The light in her window was on, and I could see Assa's silhouette against the glass. She stood at the window looking out onto the street where I was standing. I could see the dark shape where her deformed arm was. It seemed to me that she was crying. I could not see Assa's face, but because I was drunk I thought that I could see her crying. I thought that I could see the tears running down her face. Also, I thought that I was crying.

I was too drunk to notice that it was raining. Because I was drunk, I had confused the rain with tears. The rain ran down Assa's window, and the same rain soaked my hair and clothes. I had been rained on for twenty-one years, but I had never noticed it before. I stood at the end of the driveway, and the rain soaked my hair and my clothes and my skin. I felt the rain on my skin, and it was the same rain that fell on Assa's window, and the same rain that had always fallen. For that moment, I felt like something made of flesh and bone and skin, like something human.

These are the last words of "A Torn Ligament," the last short story in Daniel's collection, *The People One Knows*, which he did not live to see published. I find the passage an extraordinary evocation of a lonely young man standing in confusion on the threshold of becoming an adult; of sadness and suffering, anger and longing, a telling portrait of an emotional turning point in his—the narrator, Daniel's—life. The reader can't help but hope the moment leads to redemption, yet suspects that it might not, at least for a while.

What does a young man do, a young man accustomed to numbing his feelings of terror and sadness with alcohol, in the moment after the one in which he allows himself to feel real in his own skin? I believe the older man who wrote those autobiographical words, the Daniel I knew so briefly, as he looked back with tender regret on his young, broken self, and the young woman he hurt, was also at such a turning point. There is a yearning for recovery and relief, a keen unspoken desire for healing amid the anger and despair. And that later moment in Daniel's life could have gone either way, too. Earlier in the same short story (quoted on page 57), he wonders if the relationship between him and the young woman might have turned out differently. "I do not know. I do not know," he concludes.

But we know how Daniel's story turned out, how his life ended. Mine has gone on, and I have found a way to be happy—or sometimes just ordinarily unhappy—while bearing my sorrows. Daniel's death has cast a shadow over my life, and I have had to walk with it awhile and get used to its presence there, allow time to put it behind me, and once more give pride of place to the living souls now at the centre of my days. After much searching, stumbling, standing up, falling, and standing up to push the boulder up the hill again, I do get on with my life.

But I think of him, of course. I wish he had lived to know how to distinguish rain from tears, and to cry them, as many as he had to. I wish he had lived to learn how to feel his connections to others, to himself, without fear. To be less astonished by happiness.

I wish, more than anything, that he had lived to truly understand and accept that he was, above all—like loss and grief, love and survival—something human.

NOTES

PROLOGUE

p. 7 "... one clergyman who was called upon ..." Rev. Gordon Winch, for many years the director of the Toronto Distress Centre, told me many enlightening anecdotes about his years as a counsellor to the distressed and suicidal. It was he who counselled the attempted suicide at the Don Jail, back in the early seventies.

"... self murder ..." Alvarez, Alfred. *The Savage God.* London: Penguin Books Ltd., 1971.

p. 12 "... Even Freud expressed suicidal feelings ..." Litman, Robert E., "Sigmund Freud on Suicide," *The Psychology of Suicide.* E.S. Shneidman, N.L. Farberow, and R. Litman, eds. New York: Science House, 1970.

p. 13 Statistical and other valuable information is available in *Suicide in Canada: Update of the Report of the Task Force on Suicide in Canada,* sponsored by the Mental Health Division, Health Services Directorate, Health Programs and Services Branch, Health Canada, 1994.

p. 17 Keen, Sam. *To Love and Be Loved.* New York: Bantam, 1997.

A CLOSED DOOR

p. 26 Roth, Philip. *Portnoy's Complaint.* New York: Vintage Books, 1969.

p. 27 Cohen, Leonard. *Beautiful Losers.* Toronto: McClelland and Stewart, 1966.

p. 29 Crosbie, Lynn. *Pearl.* Concord, ON: House of Anansi Press, 1996.

Camus, Albert. *The Myth of Sisyphus.* New York: Alfred A. Knopf Inc., 1955, 1983.

DANIEL, WE HARDLY KNEW YOU

p. 40–41 Solomon, Andrew. "Anatomy of Melancholy," *New Yorker* LXXIII:42. January 12, 1998.

p. 46 Sanford, Linda T. *Strong at the Broken Places: Overcoming the Trauma of Childhood Abuse.* New York: Random House Inc., 1990.

". . . a well-regarded handbook for grief counsellors . . ." Worden, J. William, *Grief Counselling and Grief Therapy: A Handbook for the Mental Health Practitioner.* New York: Springer Publishing Inc., 1991.

p. 50 Fetherling, Janet, *Canadian Literature and Modern First Editions from the Collection of Daniel Jones*, Annex Books Catalogue 16.
Fetherling, whom Daniel had contacted about selling his books not long before his death, was understandably saddened by the loss of the engaging young collector she'd known over the years, and wanted the catalogue she published to stand as an acknowledgement of Daniel's rare passion for books. It took me almost three years after his death to enter Fetherling's Toronto shop, Annex Books. When I finally did go in, Fetherling told me that not long after Daniel's suicide, another writer and book collector had sold his books to a colleague of hers and killed himself soon after.

Since then, the two book dealers had vowed that any time a writer approached them with a proposal to sell books, they would ask questions to determine his or her emotional state. Another writer did come along wanting to sell a collection. After some probing from Fetherling, the perplexed man burst out, "What is with you book dealers wanting to know about my personal life?" He had recently been grilled by the other dealer as well. When Fetherling explained, he said, "Janet, I'm fine. Just buy my books." It was an amusing story, in its bittersweet way, and I was touched by the dealers' concern. I guess we had all learned something that might come better late than never for depressed book lovers of the future.

p. 55 Miller, Alice. *The Drama of the Gifted Child.* New York: Basic Books, 1990.

p. 67–68 Etkind, Marc. . . . *Or Not To Be: A Collection of Suicide Notes.* New York: Riverhead Books, 1997.

p. 70 Alexander, Victoria. *Words I Never Thought to Speak.* Toronto: Maxwell MacMillan Canada, 1991.

p. 76 Adam, Kenneth S. "Early Family Influences on Suicidal Behavior," *Annals New York Academy of Sciences* [Vol. 486], 1986. pp. 63–76.

p. 76–77 Shneidman, Edwin S. *The Suicidal Mind.* New York: Oxford University Press, 1996.

DOING TIME IN THE PRISON
OF MOURNING

p. 100 ". . . mothers who lose their infants . . ." Rosof, Barbara D. *The Worst Loss: How Families Heal from the Death of a Child.* New York: Henry Holt and Company, 1994.

p. 107–8 Lukas, Christopher and Seiden, Henry M. *Silent Grief: Living in the Wake of Suicide.* New York: Bantam Books, 1987.

p. 118 Kim Gernack, a native suicide-prevention worker who worked in Hobbema, Alberta, during the early nineties, gave me many thoughtful insights and descriptions of the problem of suicide in that community and how it has been dealt with. Eli Allen Wolf Tail, a crisis-intervention worker on the Blood Reserve south of Calgary, also graciously took the time to be interviewed about his work and the problems facing his people.

One hopeful document that has emerged from another native community is *Horizons of Hope: An Empowering Journey,* which details the recommendations of the Nishnawbe-Aski Nation Youth Forum on Suicide for dealing with the problem among native youth in northern Ontario.

p. 120 Govier, Katherine. "Surviving Harvey," *Toronto Life,* December 1996.

AT PLAY IN THE FIELDS OF
'THE SAVAGE GOD'

p. 127 Phillips, David P. "The Werther Effect." *The Sciences* 25:4, 1985. pp. 32–39.

p. 129 Curtis, Deborah. *Touching from a Distance.* London: Faber and Faber, 1995.

p. 130–31 Greer, Germaine. *Slip-Shod Sibyls: Recognition, Rejection and the Woman Poet.* London, England: Viking, 1995.

Alvarez. *The Savage God.*

p. 140 ". . . studies on the links . . ." Gould, Madelyn S., and Schaffer, David. "The Impact of Suicide in Television Movies: Evidence of Imitation," *New England Journal of Medicine* 315:11, 1986. pp. 690–94.

Berman, Alan L. "Fictional Depictions of Suicide in Television, Films and Imitation Effects," *American Journal of Psychiatry* 145:8, August 1988. pp. 982–86.

NOTES

TRAVELS WITH MY GRIEF

p. 150–51 Landerkin, Hon. Hugh F. *Report to the Attorney General, Public Inquiry into the death of Isaac Gerard Mercer, The Fatalities Inquiries Act, Canada, The Province of Alberta.* January 1998.

p. 153–54 Boldt, Menno. *Report of the Task Force on Suicides to The Minister of Social Services and Community Health The Honourable Helen Huntley.* May 1976.

p. 156–57 Colt, George Howe. *The Enigma of Suicide.* New York: Simon & Schuster, 1992.

STRANGERS ON THE NET

p. 179 O'Carroll, Patrick, MD, MPH. *Overcoming the Legacy of Off-line Thinking: The Internet as a Fundamental Suicide Prevention Tool.* Keynote panel presentation, 30th Annual Conference of the American Association of Suicidology. Memphis, Tennessee. April 1997.

LAST WORDS

p. 201 Camus, Albert. *The Myth of Sisyphus and Other Essays.* Justin O'Brien, trans. New York: Vantage Books, 1991.

p. 202 Parker, Dorothy. *The Collected Poetry of Dorothy Parker.* New York: Random House, 1959.

p. 205–6 Fenton, James. "For Andrew Wood," *Out of Danger.* New York: Farrar, Strauss, Giroux, 1994.

FURTHER READING

Alexander, Victoria. *Words I Never Thought to Speak: Stories of Life in the Wake of Suicide.* Toronto: Maxwell Macmillan Canada, 1991.

Alvarez, A. (Alfred). *The Savage God: A Study of Suicide.* Harmondsworth, England: Penguin Books, 1974.

Amis, Martin. *Night Train.* Toronto: Knopf, 1997.

Ayer, Eleanor H. *Teen Suicide: Is It Too Painful to Grow Up?* New York: Twenty-First Century Books, 1993.

Baechler, Jean. *Suicides.* New York: Basic Books, 1979.

Bentley Mays, John. *In the Jaws of the Black Dog: A Memoir of Depression.* Toronto: Penguin Books, 1995.

Bolton, Iris. *My Son . . . My Son . . . A Guide to Healing After Death, Loss or Suicide.* Atlanta, GA: Bolton Press Atlanta, 1983.

Burgess, Tony. *The Hellmouths of Bewdley.* Toronto: ECW Press, 1997.

Burton, Robert. *The Anatomy of Melancholy* (abridged and edited by Joan K. Peters). New York: Frederick Unger Publishing Co. Inc., 1979.

Button, Margo. *The Unhinging of Wings.* Lantzville, British Columbia: Oolichan Books, 1996.

Camus, Albert. *The Myth of Sisyphus and Other Essays* (Justin O'Brien, translator). New York: Vintage Books, 1991.

Chance, Sue. *Stronger than Death: When Suicide Touches Your Life.* New York: W.W. Norton & Company, Inc., 1992.

Chu, Paul E. *The Tragedy of Suicide: The Purpose of Earth Life.* Englewood Cliffs, N.J.: World View Press, 1992.

Clarke, James. *Silver Mercies.* Toronto: Exile Editions, 1997.

Colt, George Howe. *The Enigma of Suicide.* New York: Simon & Schuster, 1992.

Conrad, David L. *Out of the Nightmare: Recovery from Depression and Suicidal Pain.* New York: New Liberty Press, 1991.

Crosbie, Lynn. *Pearl.* Concord, ON: House of Anansi Press, 1996.

Curtis, Deborah. *Touching From a Distance.* London: Faber and Faber, 1995.

Dolce, Laura. *Suicide.* New York: Chelsea House, 1992

Durkheim, Emile. *Suicide: A Study in Sociology.* New York: 1st Free Press, 1966.

Etkind, Marc. . . . *Or Not to Be: A Collection of Suicide Notes.* New York: Riverhead Books, 1997.

Fine, Carla. *No Time to Say Goodbye: Surviving the Suicide of a Loved One.* New York: Doubleday, 1997.

Flanders, Stephen A. *Suicide.* New York: Facts on File, 1991.

Fuse, Toyomasa. *Suicide, Individual and Society.* Toronto: Canadian Scholars' Press, 1997.

Gay, Peter, ed. *The Freud Reader.* New York: W.W. Norton & Co., 1989.

Gray, Spalding. *Monster in a Box.* New York: Vintage, 1991.

Greer, Germaine. *Slip-Shod Sybils: Recognition, Rejection and the Woman Poet.* London: Viking, 1995.

Hammer, Signe. *By Her Own Hand: Memoirs of a Suicide's Daughter.* New York: Soho Press Inc., 1991.

Hughes, Ted. *Birthday Letters.* London: Faber and Faber, 1998.

Jones, Daniel. *The People One Knows.* Stratford, ON: The Mercury Press, 1994.

Keen, Sam. *To Love and Be Loved.* New York: Bantam, 1997.

Kubler-Ross, Elisabeth. *On Death and Dying.* Toronto: Maxwell Macmillan Canada, 1969.

Leenaars, Antoon, Wenckstern, Suzanne, Sakinofsky, Isaac, Dyck, Ronald J., Kral, Michael J., Bland, Roger C., eds. *Suicide in Canada.* Toronto: University of Toronto Press, 1998.

Lester, David. *Why People Kill Themselves: A 1990s Summary of Research Findings on Suicidal Behavior,* 3rd ed. New York: Charles C. Thomas Publishing, 1992.

Lukas, Christopher & Seiden, Henry M. *Silent Grief: Living in the Wake of Suicide.* New York: Bantam Books, 1990.

Maltsberger, John T., and Goldblatt, Mark J., eds. *Essential Papers On Suicide.* New York: New York University Press, 1996.

Miller, Alice. *The Drama of the Gifted Child.* New York: Basic Books, 1981.

Miller, John, ed. *On Suicide: Great Writers on the Ultimate Question.* San Francisco: Chronicle Books, 1992.

Nuland, Sherwin. *How We Die: Reflections on Life's Final Chapter.* New York: Vintage Books, 1995.

Rosof, Barbara D. *The Worst Loss: How Families Heal from the Death of a Child.* New York: Henry Holt and Company, 1994.

Sanford, Linda T. *Strong at the Broken Places: Overcoming the Trauma of Childhood Sexual Abuse.* New York: Random House, 1990.

Shneidman, Edwin S. *The Suicidal Mind.* New York: Oxford University Press, 1996.

Stone, George. *Suicide and Attempted Suicide: Methods and Consequences.* New York: Carroll and Graf, 1999.

Styron, William. *Darkness Visible: A Memoir of Madness.* New York: Random House, 1990.

Suicide in Canada: Update of the Report of the Task Force on Suicide in Canada. Sponsored by the Mental Health Division, Health Services Directorate, Health Programs and Services Branch, Health Canada, 1994.

Treadway, David C. *Dead Reckoning: A Therapist Confronts His Own Grief.* New York: Basic Books, 1996.

Worden, J. William. *Grief Counselling and Grief Therapy.* London: Tavistock Publications, 1983.

ACKNOWLEDGEMENTS

I am indebted to many good, generous people in the making of this book.

The staff of the Suicide Information and Education Centre in Calgary, Alberta, were unfailingly gracious and helpful—thank you to Deana Franssen, Gerry Harrington, and Karen Kiddey. I am also grateful to Dick Ramsey, Dr. Bryan Tanney, and the late Roger Tierney for sharing their knowledge and experience with me. Menno Boldt, Kim Gernack, and Eli Allen Wolf Tail added to my understanding during my western research forays. For their insight, I also thank Pat Harnish of the Toronto Distress Centre, Ted Kaiser of Kids Help Phone, Rabbi David Marmur of Holy Blossom Temple, and Rev. Gordon Winch, also of the Toronto Distress Centre.

I also gratefully acknowledge the financial support of The Canada Council.

Invaluable help and friendship has come from Hilde Schlosar of the Samaritans of Southern Alberta; thank you as well to Wayne Carlson, and the Sams of Drum Pen.

Karen Letofsky's rare combination of warmth and wisdom guided me through the healing and writing process, and kept me from heading down a few dead ends and mistaken pathways. I come away from all our conversations feeling I have gained new and deeper perspective.

For sharing painful personal stories, I particularly thank Norma Beattie, Don and Brenda Ebbitt, Wendy Lemon, Ken Mercer, Karen and Bruce Payne, and Debbie Roulette. I also thank those who asked to remain anonymous: Your reflections enlightened me greatly, and inform this book.

I would especially like to acknowledge and thank, for their encouragement, support, insights, suggestions, clippings, and many random acts of kindness: Oona Ajzenstat, André Alexis,

Doug Bell, Dan Bortolotti, Tony Burgess, Theresa Burke, June Callwood, Jeffrey Canton, Cathy Collins, Kevin Connolly, the late Jim Cormier, Irene Cox, Lynn Crosbie, Lynn Cunningham, Andrea Curtis, Dr. William Davies, Connie da Silva Borges, Tim Falconer, Alyse Frampton, Ena Fry, Rachel Giese, Nora Gold, Phil Hall, Fern Hawker, Karen Heiber, Lynne Hussey, Kathleen Johnson, Norma and Roger Jones, Joe Kary, M. T. Kelly, Gordon Laird, Jackie, Lisa and Bill MacTaggart, Jeannie Marshall, Nancy Metcalfe, Daisy Moore, Dr. Frances Newman, Don Obe, Grainne O'Donnell, Sheree Lee Olson, Zdravko Planinc, Dr. Dinah Power, Scott Proudfoot, Alexandra Radkewycz, Pat Rakabowchuk, Laima Reiner, Norman Ringel, Rick Salutin, Bruce Serafin, Clare and Alan Thomas, Clive Thompson, Jane Willis, and Morris Wolfe.

A huge thank you to Iris Tupholme, for knowing what this book could be from the beginning, and letting it happen; also to Karen Hanson, for fine editing, and to Kathleen Richards, for her suggestions and eagle eye.

Special thanks to my sister, Jeannie Farr, and to Jo Robertson, for love and support in times that were rough on all of us. I also thank my father, Vince Farr.

For reconnecting me with many natural wonders, I am grateful to patient, happy-spirited Tony Beck.

Whenever I read the following passage from James Fenton's poem, "For Andrew Wood," from the collection *Out of Danger*, I give thanks for my enduring friendships. I also think of Daniel. I offer this in memory of him.

And so the dead might cease to grieve
And we might make amends
And there might be a pact between
Dead friends and living friends
What our dead friends would want from us
Would be such living friends

EXCERPTS